Series II

LECTIONARY

Worship Aids
Cycle A

FOR USE WITH THE
COMMON LECTIONARY

PAUL A. LAUGHLIN

C.S.S. Publishing Co., Inc.
Lima, Ohio

LECTIONARY WORSHIP AIDS A, SERIES II

Copyright © 1989 by
The C.S.S. Publishing Company, Inc.
Lima, Ohio

You may copy the material in this publication if you are the original purchaser, for use as it was intended (worship material for worship use; educational material for classroom use; dramatic material for staging and production). No additional permission is required from the publisher for such copying by the original purchaser only. Inquiries should be addressed to: The C.S.S. Publishing Company, Inc., 628 South Main Street, Lima, Ohio 45804.

Library of Congress Cataloging-in-Publication Data
(Revised for volume 2)

Laughlin, Paul A., 1946-
  Lectionary worship aids, series II.

  Spine title: Worship aids.
  Includes index.
  Contents: [1] Cycle B — [2] Cycle A.
  1. Common lectionary. 2. Worship programs. I. Title
BV198.L37   1989   264'.34   87-6314
ISBN 0-8953-6886-2 (pkb. : v. 1)

9863 / ISBN 1-55673-138-8   PRINTED IN U.S.A.

To my little poet —

*Charming
angel,
never stop
dancing,
and
channeling
eternity*

*"Angels can fly
because
they take themselves
lightly."*

—*G. K. Chesterton*

Table of Contents

Introduction 6

The Season of Advent

First Sunday in Advent 9
Second Sunday in Advent 12
Third Sunday in Advent 15
Fourth Sunday in Advent 18

The Season of Christmas

Christmas Eve/Day (First Proper) 21
Christmas Eve/Day (Second Proper) 24
Christmas Eve/Day (Third Proper) 27
First Sunday after Christmas (Holy Family) 30
The Holy Name of Jesus (January 1) 33
Second Sunday after Christmas 36

The Season of Epiphany

The Epiphany of Our Lord (January 6) 39
The Baptism of Our Lord (First Sunday after the Epiphany) . 42
Second Sunday after the Epiphany 45
Third Sunday after the Epiphany 48
Fourth Sunday after the Epiphany 51
Fifth Sunday after the Epiphany 54
Sixth Sunday after the Epiphany 57
Seventh Sunday after the Epiphany 60
Eighth Sunday after the Epiphany 63
The Transfiguration of Our Lord 66

The Season of Lent

Ash Wednesday 69
The First Sunday in Lent 72
The Second Sunday in Lent 75
The Third Sunday in Lent 78
The Fourth Sunday in Lent 81
The Fifth Sunday in Lent 84
The Sixth Sunday in Lent (observed as Passion Sunday) ... 87
The Sixth Sunday in Lent (observed as Palm Sunday) 90
    Monday in Holy Week 93
    Tuesday in Holy Week 96
    Wednesday in Holy Week 99
    Maundy Thursday in Holy Week 102
    Good Friday 105

The Season of Easter

The Resurrection of Our Lord (Easter Day) 108
The Second Sunday of Easter 111
The Third Sunday of Easter 114
The Fourth Sunday of Easter 117
The Fifth Sunday of Easter 120
The Sixth Sunday of Easter 123
Ascension Day/Ascension Sunday 126
The Seventh Sunday of Easter 129
The Day of Pentecost 132

The Time of the Church
The Season after Pentecost

The Holy Trinity (The First Sunday after Pentecost) 135
Proper 4   (May 29—June 4) 138
Proper 5   (June 5-11) 141
Proper 6   (June 12-18) 144
Proper 7   (June 19-25) 147
Proper 8   (June 26—July 2) 150
Proper 9   (July 3-9) 153
Proper 10 (July 10-16) 156
Proper 11 (July 17-23) 159
Proper 12 (July 24-30) 162
Proper 13 (July 31—August 6) 165
Proper 14 (August 7-13) 168
Proper 15 (August 14-20) 171
Proper 16 (August 21-27) 174
Proper 17 (August 28—September 3) 177
Proper 18 (September 4-10) 180
Proper 19 (September 11-17) 183
Proper 20 (September 18-24) 186
Proper 21 (September 25—October 1) 189
Proper 22 (October 2-8) 192
Proper 23 (October 9-15) 195
Proper 24 (October 16-22) 198
Proper 25 (October 23-29) 201
Proper 26 (October 30—November 5) 204
Proper 27 (November 6-12) 207
Proper 28 (November 13-19) 210
Proper 29 (November 20-26) 213

All Saints' Day/All Saints' Sunday 216
Thanksgiving Day 219

Scripture Index 222
About the Author 226

Introduction

This first of three volumes in Series II of *Lectionary Worship Aids* is actually the third written, since I began the project at mid-point with Cycle B, followed that with Cycle C, and now complete the series with Cycle A. I am able, therefore, to view the whole trilogy in its entirety from the standpoint of this first volume, not with clairvoyance, but with what biblical scholars call *vaticinium ex eventu* — prophecy after the fact.

The format of all three volumes is the same. The designated lections are from the consensus lectionary developed by the North American Committee on Calendar and Lectionary of the Consultation on Church Union, which is widely used today. I have suggested a theme for each passage, and provided an exegetical note to indicate just how the theme derives from the text. I have then tried to carry my suggested theme, which is always only one among many possible, very deliberately through a call to worship, a collect, and a prayer of confession. I have endeavored (particularly in the two most recent volumes) to base many of the calls to worship upon the Responsorial Psalms prescribed by the consensus lectionary, but I have taken liberties in excerpting, interpreting, and wording these psalms, in an effort to remain true to their original intent while avoiding a mere parroting of them. Occasionally I have used portions of the prescribed psalm not included in the lection.

As always, I recommend that the user of this volume take nothing in it at face value, but tailor the material to personal and local sensitivities and needs. I would especially point out that the exegetical notes are just that: notes. They are, at best, clues to the direction or angle on the scriptural text from which I drew the suggested theme and upon which I constructed the prayers. Such scant, suggestive notes are no substitute for real, thoroughgoing, informed exegesis on the part of the user. I would also recommend that all of the texts for each given day be examined carefully, so that common or complementary themes might be discovered of a sort that the serial format of these volumes may tend to obscure. If, after all, my material provokes a user to take an entirely different approach from my own to one or all of the lections, I am pleased to have been a part of the process. That kind of independence, when exhibited in students, is a professor's dream-come-true!

For the theological rationale for these volumes I would direct the reader's attention to the introduction to my Cycle C volume. As far as I can tell, there has been no dramatic change in Christian doctrine, the modern theological landscape, or my own views since I penned that essay; and I have been assured by people whose opinions I value that what I say there is a reasonably accurate assessment of the problematic conceptual context in which Christian liturgy and its language must be forged in the late 20th century. There is no need to replicate those remarks here. Suffice it to say that throughout my work on this series I have been surprised, frustrated, and sometimes dismayed by the theological demands of conceiving liturgy within the constraints, not only of the lectionary, but of the canon as well. For all their many virtues, both are still historically and culturally conditioned and therefore reflective of the male-dominated, hierarchical, and dualistic thinking about God and God's relation to the world and humanity that classic Judaeo-Christian theism historically has spawned. To some extent, the liturgical year itself, as traditionally and presently conceived, compounds the difficulty. For as long as it culminates in a festival of "Christ the King" (to cite but one example) the movement toward both inclusive and egalitarian imagery will be incomplete. I decided early on that a series like this is not the proper forum in which to address such basic theological issues, so I have attempted in the following pages to remain within the theistic structure that forms the backdrop to the Bible and traditional Christian theology, rather than to challenge it in any significant way. I have made a concerted effort in all three volumes, however, with varying success, to use inclusive language for both God and humanity. Yet the images in some of the biblical passages prescribed by the lectionary seem too intractably masculine, monarchical, and militaristic to modern sensitivities to be redeemable by mere word-play. If some of these images appear in the pages of this series, it is because I felt constrained by the lectionary to use them.

    Despite my theological and linguistic struggles with the prescribed lections throughout my work on this series, however, I am more convinced than ever of the propriety of keeping (or relocating!) the canonical scriptures at the center of Christian worship, and of the importance of a lectionary in directing their use. For, as a teacher, I believe that most real insight, learning, and growth come through creative dissonance and tension between one's beliefs and incongruous views, particularly ancient ones. I know that my own confrontations with the sometimes inhospitable nature of many of the prescribed readings have forced me time and again to clarify my own theology, often more by contradiction than by agreement. Had I been given the license, which some Christian denominations commend, of simply building themes on passages that I had selected, these three volumes would have been more about me and my theology than about the Bible and the rich, if sometimes problematic,

Christian doctrine that it has underpinned. My intention here was to allow the user to be challenged to clarify her or his perspective in preparing the actual worship service through precisely the kinds of tensions that I experienced in the production of these pages.

Now that the series is completed, I would like to thank my colleague and friend, Dr. James B. Recob, Chairperson of the Department of Religion and Philosophy at Otterbein College, and the Reverend Larry Hard, formerly of nearby Church of the Messiah (United Methodist) in Westerville, Ohio, for recommending me for this project in the first place. I am also grateful to Otterbein College for permitting me to devote a sabbatical leave and additional release time to the completion of two of these volumes. I continue to be indebted to all of those mentioned in the other two volumes as having assisted me with their comments and criticisms. And finally, I am deeply beholden, and dedicate this volume, to my little angelic poet, who, in lieu of a muse, kept me in touch with my sometimes subliminal spirituality.

Paul A. Laughlin
Otterbein College
Lent, 1989

First Sunday in Advent

First Lesson: Isaiah 2:1-5

Theme: Universal peace from God's unitive power

Exegetical note: This eschatological ("latter days") vision, the core of which also appears in the opening verses of Micah 4, makes the temple site at Jerusalem ("the mountain of the house of God") a kind of magnetic pole, to which all nations of the world will be inexorably drawn for (1) instruction in righteousness, (2) political arbitration, and (3) lasting peace — all under God's power.

Call to Worship
(based on Psalm 122)

Leader: Let us be glad to be at the house of God!

People: LET US REJOICE AND GIVE THANKS TO GOD'S HOLY NAME!

Leader: For the house of God is a place of divine judgment!

People: AND THE HOUSE OF GOD IS A PLACE OF LASTING PEACE!

Collect

Righteous God, you have established your holy city and all your houses throughout the world as havens of divine instruction and safe harbors of peace. Enable us to ease all tensions and strife, especially between nations and races and creeds: that your divine and universal love may triumph and war and hatred may cease. In the name of the coming Prince of Peace we pray. Amen

Prayer of Confession

God of Peace, we confess with deep sadness that we do not always operate as coworkers with you in the enterprise of world peace, but instead sow the seeds of lasting discord with our prejudices, our stereotypes, our jokes, and even our blind and uncritical patriotism. Forgive us, we pray, draw us to your divine will, instruct us in your holy ways, and make us more worthy bearers of the name of the One who comes in Peace. In his name we pray. Amen

First Sunday in Advent

Second Lesson: Romans 13:11-14

Theme: The Christian's place on "the edge of night"

Exegetical note: Notwithstanding the non-occurrence (or "delay") of the second coming of Christ, which Paul and his followers saw as imminent, references in these hortatory verses to an "hour" and "full time" provide a new slant on the effect of the "first" coming, namely, that, with the "dawning" of this "new light," the Christian stands "on the edge of night," surrounded by but awakened from the "darkness" and the evil works that it has veiled.

Call to Worship

Leader: Arise from darkness, Christians, and face the Light!

People: FOR THE BIRTH OF CHRIST IS THE DAWN OF A NEW AGE!

Leader: Awake from sleep, Christians, and behold the new day!

People: FOR, THOUGH YET SURROUNDED BY NIGHT, WE MAY NOW LIVE IN THE GLOW OF THE RISING SON!

Collect

Radiant God, you sent Jesus to illumine a world darkened by evil and sin. Point us toward his Light: that, our faces warmed and brightened by the dawn he brings, we may live redeemed lives of purity and love, even though we still can feel the cold darkness of the passing evil age on our backs. Yearning for the coming of your Light we pray. Amen

Prayer of Confession

God of Light, it saddens us deeply to realize how much and how often we succumb to the spiritual darkness that surrounds us, despair over the evil that assails us, and fail to look in hope and anticipation toward the bright dawning of your Reign and the coming of your Christ. Forgive us, O God, and transform us into true children of Light in the image and likeness of Jesus. In his name we pray. Amen

First Sunday in Advent

Gospel: Matthew 24:36-44

Theme: God's reliable unpredictability

Exegetical note: This passage comes toward the end of Matthew's version of the "Little Apocalypse" in Mark 13 and, like its source, emphasizes the unpredictability of the expected and desired parousia, and the consequent need for watchfulness and readiness. For Advent, the passage provides an excellent reminder that, despite the reliability of God's promises, God acts in God's own good time, and therefore predictions and pronouncements about when (or, for that matter, how) God may or may not act in the future are, at best, imprudent.

Call to Worship

Leader: Watch, sisters and brothers, for the doings of God are always a surprise!

People: GOD GRANTS US GRACE IN GOD'S GOOD TIME!

Leader: Be ready, Christians, for the comings of the Christ are always unexpected!

People: THAT THE CHRIST COMES IS A CERTAINTY; WHEN THE CHRIST COMES IS A MYSTERY!

Collect

God of saving surprises, you sent a Christ who caught off guard even those who anticipated and expected him, and showered your grace in ways no one could have foreseen. Make us ready and watchful: that, whenever your unprecedented and unpredictable acts of redemption do come upon us, we may be open and receptive to all of their benefits. In the name of the coming Christ we pray. Amen

Prayer of Confession

God of reliable mercy, we confess that we often try to anticipate your acts of redemption and to figure out what your future holds, and that we wind up entrusting our destinies to our guesses rather than to your graces. Forgive us our presumption, we pray, and teach us to look for the kind of surprises that you presented in the coming of the Christ. In his holy name we pray. Amen

Second Sunday in Advent

First Lesson: Isaiah 11:1-10

Theme: The qualities and consequences of the One who comes

Exegetical note: This description of the ideal Davidic king (i.e., the hoped-for Messiah) contains three pairs of desired qualities: wisdom and understanding (intellectual), counsel and might (political), and knowledge and fear of God (spiritual). All of these derive, not from the ruler's innate abilities, but from the Spirit of God that will be upon him; and the righteousness that will "gird" him will bias him toward the poor and the meek, and will lead to a paradisal, peaceful state that will affect, not only Israel ("my holy mountain"), but indeed the world.

Call to Worship
(based on Psalm 72)

Leader: May God's chosen One come in justice!

People: MAY GOD'S APPOINTED ONE COME IN RIGHTEOUSNESS!

Leader: May God's Messiah defend the poor and deliver the needy!

People: MAY GOD'S MESSIAH BRING PROSPERITY TO US ALL!

Collect

God of consummate justice, you promised a ruler of wisdom and understanding, of counsel and might, of knowledge and fear of you, one full of your Spirit and clothed in your righteousness. Help us to see this hope fulfilled in the coming Christ: that, inspired by these godly characteristics, we too may see their consequences — a world of peace. In the name of Jesus we pray. Amen

Prayer of Confession

Most compassionate judge, it grieves us to recognize how seldom we exhibit the passion for justice and righteousness or the concern for the poor and downtrodden that your prophets consistently attribute to the coming Messiah and Messianic Reign. Forgive us, we pray, and teach us to trade our self-serving and selfish hopes for ones worthy of the coming Christ, in whose name we pray. Amen

Second Sunday in Advent

Second Lesson: Romans 15:4-13

Theme: The Christ's coming and Christian confidence

Exegetical note: Paul's exhortation here to Christian unity and harmony, especially between Gentile and Jew, is framed by the idea of hope. (vv. 4 and 13) The phrase "whatever was written in former days" means the Jewish canon (the Christian Old Testament), which he takes as a source of hope because of its reflection of the "steadfastness and encouragement of God" as confirmed in Jesus' mission of servanthood, in which all Christians may take confidence.

Call to Worship
(based on Psalm 72)

Leader: May the one who comes endure like the sun!

People: MAY THE ONE WHO COMES BE AS LASTING AS THE MOON!

Leader: May the Christ of God be like showers that water the earth!

People: MAY THE CHRIST OF GOD BRING RIGHTEOUSNESS AND PEACE!

Collect

God of abundant promises, you fulfilled the hopes of Israel and the yearnings of the prophets for a Messiah in a surprising way that none of us could have anticipated. Give us at least the wisdom of hindsight: that, recognizing in Jesus the Christ, we may learn once again to place our trust in your promises and our confidence in your word. In the name of the Coming Christ we pray. Amen

Prayer of Confession

All-compassionate God, we confess with sorrow how quickly and completely we lose confidence in you and your promises for righteousness and peace, and fall into despair over our decadent world and its dismal prospects. Forgive us, we pray, and set before us the image of Jesus, the coming Christ, so that we may learn through him and his mission of servanthood to trust at last in you and to hope in your everlasting Reign. In his name we pray. Amen

Dec. 10th

Second Sunday in Advent

Gospel: Matthew 3:1-12

Theme: Beyond nativity

Exegetical note: The enigmatic and eccentric figure of John the Baptizer is rich and colorful in this passage and elsewhere in the New Testament, but for this Sunday the real focus of attention should be the coming One whom he proclaims. In this regard, it is noteworthy that the "coming" to which John refers is not Jesus' birth but his ministry, a helpful reminder in this season that the advent we celebrate is more than just a nativity; it is a life, a ministry, and even a death.

Call to Worship

Leader: Repent, Christians, for the Reign of God is at hand!

People: HEAR THE VOICE IN THE WILDERNESS PROCLAIMING ITS NEARNESS!

Leader: John the Baptizer was great, but Jesus the baptized was greater!

People: FOR, BAPTIZED WITH WATER, HE BAPTIZED WITH THE SPIRIT AND FIRE!

Collect

Most exalted God, you sent us prophets, a baptizer, and a Christ for our redemption. Expand our vision this Advent season beyond the sentimentalities of stable and manger: that, seeing Jesus' mission, message, and ministry in its fullness, we may appreciate all there is to await and anticipate in the coming One, in whose name we pray. Amen

Prayer of Confession

God of empathy and care, we admit that we fall easily into the yearly trap of sentimentalizing the birth of Jesus for our own emotional satisfaction, and lose sight of the wonderfully tragic and redemptive life that lay beyond it. Forgive us, we pray, and help us to see that the Coming Christ for whom we prepare is more than just a baby, but indeed a baptizer with fire and the bearer of a holy Reign. In his name we pray. Amen

Third Sunday in Advent

First Lesson: Isaiah 35:1-10

Theme: Divine majesty and desert miracles

Exegetical note: In a passage reminiscent of Deutero-Isaiah (chapters 40-55), the author here celebrates the return of his people from Babylonian captivity to Jerusalem. The allusion throughout is to the earlier Exodus from Egypt, but the miracles are even greater: the desert itself is transformed by the glory and majesty of God, while the ransomed and redeemed walk the "holy way" there in wholeness, peace, and joy. From a Christian perspective, the passage prefigures the miraculous ministry of the later "divine Way," Jesus.

Call to Worship
(based on Psalm 146)

Leader: Let us praise God!

People: LET US LIFT OUR SOULS IN ADORATION!

Leader: Let us praise God as long as we live!

People: LET US PRAISE GOD AS LONG AS WE HAVE BREATH!

Collect

God of glorious splendor, you have time and again led your people out of freedom-negating captivity, through life-threatening deserts, and into health-restoring safety. Prepare us to receive Jesus as your miraculous Way to salvation: that, seeing in him your wondrous works, we may become travelers on a holy journey toward wholeness and peace. Amen

Prayer of Confession

God of gracious sensitivity, we confess that we tend to resign ourselves to the captivities and deserts of life, and fail to avail ourselves of the holy ways to freedom and life, wholeness and peace that you continually provide, especially in the coming Christ. Forgive us, we pray, and help us this Advent season to prepare ourselves for the holy Way that leads to restoration, renewal, and redemption. In his name we pray. Amen

Third Sunday in Advent

Second Lesson: James 5:7-10

Theme: Advent as judgment

Exegetical note: This exhortation to patience, directed almost certainly toward the faithful poor, must be read in light of the preceding six verses, which portend the suffering of the rich. The occasion of both the urging and the warning is the *parousia* of Jesus (the Greek word appears in vv. 7 and 8), which the author takes to be "at hand." (v. 8) The focal aspect of this "coming" here is the judgment that it will bring; indeed, the one who comes is "the Judge."

Call to Worship
(based on Psalm 146)

Leader: Happy are those whose hope is in God!

People: HAPPY ARE THOSE WHO FIND HELP IN GOD!

Leader: For God created all and is faithful to the end!

People: AND GOD BRINGS JUSTICE TO THE OPPRESSED AND FOOD TO THE HUNGRY!

Collect

Magnificent God, you have set before us the hope that one will come to establish your holy Rule over a troubled world. Remind us that he brings more than just "sweetness and light": that, made aware that the Christ event means not only justification for the righteous but judgment for the unjust, we may consciously side as he did with the poor and the meek. Amen

Prayer of Confession

Merciful God, we confess that we continually lose sight of your bias toward the poor, the oppressed, the needy, the hungry, and the dispossessed, and try our best to make your gospel a comfort even to those upon whom Jesus pronounced "woes." Forgive us, we pray, and help us to adopt your attitude of concern and compassion for those who, according to Jesus, will inherit an earth renewed by your holy Reign. In his name we pray. Amen

Third Sunday in Advent

Gospel: Matthew 11:2-11

Theme: An Advent of healing

Exegetical note: Though John has already strongly implied (3:14) that Jesus is indeed "he who is to come," i.e., the Messiah, what he had heard in prison of "the deeds of the Christ" (v. 2) may have given him second thoughts by not fitting his own expectations of messianic might and judgment. In any case, Jesus' answer to the Baptizer's question is indirect: he points to his miracles, phrasing them not so much to showcase his own identity or powers (much less divinity) as to indicate God's healing activity in his ministry.

Call to Worship
(based on Psalm 146)

Leader: Let us praise the God who sets prisoners free!

People: LET US PRAISE THE GOD WHO GIVES SIGHT TO THE BLIND!

Leader: Our God uplifts the oppressed!

People: OUR GOD WATCHES OVER THE VULNERABLE!

Collect

God of holiness, you have laid upon the hearts and minds of your people great expectations about the justice and peace your coming Christ will bring. Inspire us again with the miraculous deeds of Jesus: that, moved by the healing that marked his ministry, we too may become agents for the alleviation of pain and suffering in our battered and broken world. Amen

Prayer of Confession

God of wholeness, we confess that we have avoided responsibility by misusing and mistaking the stories of Jesus' miracles as proofs of some abstract doctrines about his uniqueness rather than as signs of your presence and power, and indications of what we, too, should be doing in the world. Forgive us, we pray, and teach us as bearers of the name of the Christ to mirror his ministry with healing acts of our own, however modest they may be. In that name we pray. Amen

Fourth Sunday in Advent

First Lesson: Isaiah 7:10-16

Theme: Our futile present vs. God's future presence

Exegetical note: In its original setting, this famous prophecy was directed at a reluctant recipient, King Ahaz of Judah, and promised him, despite the seeming futility of his present political situation, a sign of eventual success over his enemies in the person of one to be born to a girl (*almah*) and to be named, symbolically, "God with us." The passage reflects the Old Testament pattern of promising future divine presence and providence to the hard-pressed, and to that extent points to Jesus as a medium of God's saving activity.

Call to Worship
(based on Psalm 24)

Leader: The earth is God's in all its fullness!

People: THE WORLD AND ALL ITS INHABITANTS BELONG TO GOD!

Leader: For God founded it upon the seas!

People: GOD ESTABLISHED IT UPON THE FLOODS!

Collect

God of holy power, you have always set the prospects of your marvelous future presence before those whose present seemed futile. Persuade us with your promises to expect great things: that, seeing beyond our own limited possibilities and powers, we may look in hope to a time when you will bring redemption and peace once and for all to this troubled world. Amen

Prayer of Confession

God of heavenly presence, it shames us to admit how difficult we find it to look beyond the defects of the present age and to generate hope even in your power to redeem and restore. Forgive us our scepticism and cynicism, and move us with the image of Jesus, who came, comes, and will certainly come again as Immanuel, "God with us," bringing the unity, wholeness love, and peace that only you and your grace can give. In his holy name we pray. Amen

Fourth Sunday in Advent

Second Lesson: Romans 1:1-7

Theme: Holy power in a humble person

Exegetical note: In the longest of all of his epistolary salutations, Paul here provides the Roman Christians, whom he had not yet visited, with a concise compendium of his Christology. Its heart is the parallel construction in vv. 3 and 4, which sets Jesus' fleshly descendency from David over against his spiritual "designation" as Son of God "by his resurrection from the dead." The wording of the latter component of this parallel is especially ambiguous, and at least hints of "adoptionist" sentiments. But the real point withal seems to be the contrast between the power of the resurrected Christ and the humility of his earthly life.

Call to Worship
(based on Psalm 24)

Leader: Lift up your heads, O gates!

People: BE LIFTED UP EVERLASTING DOORS!

Leader: That the God of glory may enter!

People: THAT THE GOD OF HOSTS MAY BE PRAISED!

Collect

Wondrous God, you stunned the world by hiding your majesty in a person lowly born and modestly reared. Attune us to your surprising ways of salvation: that, impressed with the image of one manger-born, we may seek you in the least and lowliest, the meekest and the mildest, the most humble and human. In Jesus' name we pray. Amen

Prayer of Confession

Wonder-working God, we confess that we tend to reverse the miracle of the Incarnation in our own lives: instead of reflecting Jesus' humility in his earthly life, and hoping for a measure of his resurrection power, we seek worldly power, prestige, and possessions in this life, and virtually ignore the promises of life eternal offered to us by your grace. Forgive us, we pray, and transform us into the image of the Christ, in whose name we pray. Amen

Fourth Sunday in Advent

Gospel: Matthew 1:18-25

Theme: God's disruptive agenda

Exegetical note: Matthew's purpose in this well-known passage is theological rather than genealogical, not to prove Jesus' divinity, however, but only his fulfillment of Isaiah 7:14. To what extent the tradition about this miraculous conception was influenced, or even generated by the Greek Septuagint's rendering of the Hebrew *almah* as *parthenos* is unclear. But the real focus of this account is Joseph and his willingness to set aside his deeply-ingrained moral standards and best-laid plans in order to cooperate in God's extraordinary (and disruptive!) agenda.

Call to Worship

Leader: Rejoice, Christians, for the Christ is at hand!

People: LET US TURN OUR EYES TO GOD'S FUTURE, WHICH STRETCHES BEFORE US!

Leader: Let us worship the God whose grace violates our standards!

People: LET US WORSHIP THE GOD WHOSE LOVE DISRUPTS OUR PLANS!

Collect

Creative God, throughout history you have taken people unawares and unsettled them with your extraordinary acts. Open us to your unpredictable workings: that, when confronted with divine activity, we shall be more ready and willing to set aside our petty plans and priorities for your grand and gracious goals. In the name of the Virgin-born we pray. Amen

Prayer of Confession

Caring God, we confess how often we let our values and standards, plans and objectives rule our lives, and our reluctance to let them be interrupted, even by your gracious interventions. Forgive us, we pray, and make us more alert and receptive to the many times you attempt to intrude into our pedestrian lives with redemptive events. Mindful of One of exceptional birth we pray. Amen

Christmas, First Proper
(Christmas Eve/Day)

First Lesson: Isaiah 9:2-7

Theme: The power of God's presence

Exegetical note: This joyous coronation anthem probably celebrated the enthronement rather than the actual birth of a new Davidic King of Judah (perhaps Hezekiah) and expressed the messianic hope that this would at last be the one to restore both prosperity and security to God's people. That this hymn takes the extraordinary license of addressing this new king as "Mighty God" indicates that the people saw in this quasi-birth event the power of God's very presence. As applied in Christian retrospect to Jesus' actual birth, the poem provides a Hebrew-historical (rather than a Greek-metaphysical) understanding of the newborn's divinity.

Call to Worship
(based on Psalm 96)

Leader: O sing a new song to God all the earth!

People: LET ALL THE WORLD SING BLESSINGS FOR GOD'S SALVATION!

Leader: Declare God's glory among the nations!

People: LET US PROCLAIM GOD'S POWERFUL ACTS TO ALL PEOPLES!

Collect

God of might, you have shared with us the power of your presence in one lowly-born this day. Prepare our spirits to receive this great gift again: that, behind the sweet new humanity of this special child, we may see and sense your very divinity, and may declare with the first Christians "God with us!" In his name we pray. Amen

Prayer of Confession

God of mercy, we confess that we have often conceived of the divinity of the Christ-child in ways that have distanced him from us instead of bringing you close. Forgive us, we pray, and help us to use this day as an opportunity to feel anew your power and presence, your glory and grace, your divinity and humanity. In the name of the Christ-child we pray. Amen

Christmas, First Proper
(Christmas Eve/Day)

Second Lesson: Titus 2:11-14

Theme: The consequences of Christmas

Exegetical note: In this brief doctrinal incursion into an otherwise largely hortatory letter, "the grace of God" refers to the first coming of the Christ, and "the glory of God" to the second. The author, almost certainly not Paul and very probably not even Jewish, at least manages to capture one dynamic of his namesake's theology in his assertion that godly lives and eagerness to do good deeds are practical consequences of such theophanies and the salvation that they bring, and are not themselves the source of redemption.

Call to Worship
(based on Psalm 96)

Leader: Great is our God, and greatly to be praised!

People: FOR ALL OTHER GODS ARE MERE IDOLS!

Leader: Honor and majesty belong to our God!

People: STRENGTH AND BEAUTY GRACE GOD'S SANCTUARY!

Collect

God of glory, you have graced us this day with your honor and majesty hidden in the humility and modesty of a stable manger. Fill us again with the wonder of this event: that, moved once more by the fullness of your gift in the newborn Christ, we may live godly lives of good works. In his name we pray. Amen

Prayer of Confession

God of grace, we know and regret that we have failed miserably to express the consequences of the Christmas event with lives that reflect the salvation that it brings. Forgive us, we pray, and empower us with your Holy Spirit, to the end that our words and our works, our attitudes and our actions may reflect the purity and perfection of the blessed baby whose birth we celebrate this day. Amen

Christmas, First Proper
(Christmas Eve/Day)

Gospel: Luke 2:1-20

Theme: God's gracious good will

Exegetical note: Luke's nativity narrative is rich, picturesque, imaginative, and (above all) symbolic. Among the many explorable details is an often misunderstood phrase, which comes as a part of the angelic multitude's hymn, namely, the declaration of peace among "men," either those "of good will" or those "with whom God is pleased." The latter probably comes closer to the original intent of the idiomatic text, and makes the sound theological point that the benefits of this whole event derive from God's gracious good will, not from human merit.

Call to Worship
(based on Psalm 96)

Leader: Let the heavens be glad! Let the earth rejoice!

People: LET THE SEA ROAR, AND ALL THAT ARE IN IT!

Leader: Let the fields celebrate, and all that inhabit it!

People: FOR GOD COMES TO REIGN! HALLELUJAH!

Collect

Most high God, you sent angels with a message of peace for humanity through your good will. Make us attentive to that proclamation: that, hearing in it a declaration of your gracious love and forgiveness, we may become the men and women of good will that you would have us to be. In gratitude for the Christ child we pray. Amen

Prayer of Confession

God of loving kindness, we acknowledge with deep sorrow our regrettable and selfish tendency to mis-hear the glad tidings of great joy, and to think that the good news is ours because we are people of good will. Forgive us, we pray, and convince us once and for all that the good will that brings the message of peace is yours, and that it is intended for all. Make us truly benevolent by your grace. In the name of Emmanuel, who comes this day, we pray. Amen

Christmas, Second Prayer
(Christmas Eve/Day)

First Lesson: Isaiah 62:6-7, 10-12

Theme: God's coming salvation

Exegetical note: These verses are drawn from a larger passage that announces the imminent restoration of Judah, and particularly Jerusalem, after the fall of Babylon. The central eschatological announcement in verse 11 — "Behold your salvation comes" — and the accompanying assertion that God's people will be remembered and redeemed rather than forsaken and forgotten are as appropriate for the new people of God (the Church) as for the old (Israel).

Call to Worship
(based on Psalm 97)

Leader: Let the earth rejoice, for God reigns!

People: THE FOUNDATIONS OF GOD'S THRONE ARE JUSTICE AND RIGHTEOUSNESS!

Leader: Clouds and darkness surround our God!

People: BUT GOD'S LIGHTNINGS LIGHTEN THE EARTH!

Collect

Reigning God, you have announced through prophets and angels your regard and redemption for those who feel most forgotten and forsaken. Let us again hear their blessed proclamations: that, touched by the promises of your powerful presence in the world, we may be filled with hope and moved to love in the name of him whose nativity we celebrate today. Amen

Prayer of Confession

Redeeming God, we confess that we often succumb to feelings of Godforsakenness, with respect to ourselves and our world; and that we lose both faith in you and hope in your promises. Forgive us, we pray, and let the words of your holy scriptures and the workings of your Holy Spirit revive and restore in us the conviction that our salvation does indeed come, in the person of the One who is born this day. In his holy name we pray. Amen

Christmas, Second Proper
(Christmas Eve/Day)

Second Lesson: Titus 3:4-7

Theme: Heirs by grace and mercy, not goodness and merit

Exegetical note: This doctrinal incursion into an otherwise largely ethical discourse states a central theme in Paul's theology, namely, that salvation comes by God's grace and mercy rather than by human goodness and merit. What is added here is the notion that, as a result of God's initiative in outpouring the Holy Spirit in the Christ, the recipients are, in effect, adopted as children who are destined to inherit eternal life.

Call to Worship
(based on Psalm 97)

Leader: Let the heavens declare God's righteousness!

People: LET ALL PEOPLE BEHOLD GOD'S GLORY!

Leader: All gods bow before our God!

People: AND ALL IDOLS SHATTER IN SHAME!

Collect

Almighty God, you have given us your Son Jesus to share our human nature from cradle to grave. Grant that we also may be made children of yours by your grace and mercy in him: that, thus reborn and renewed, we shall truly become heirs of eternal life. In the name of the newborn Savior we pray. Amen

Prayer of Confession

All-merciful God, it grieves us deeply to admit how much we still depend upon the illusion of our own goodness and merit for our salvation, rather than the reality of your grace and mercy, and come to expect eternal life as a reward rather than a gift. Forgive us, we pray, and teach us always to rely upon your loving kindness, which alone makes us children of yours and sisters and brothers of the holy One who is born today. In his precious name we pray. Amen

Christmas, Second Proper
(Christmas Eve/Day)

Gospel: Luke 2:8-20

Theme: The Christ-child as a sign of salvation

Exegetical note: The humble shepherds are directed to the swaddled child in the lowly manger by an angel messenger, who tells them, not that he is the expected messianic Savior, but only that their finding him will be a "sign" of the arrival of the Christ. That indirect way of designating the identity of the baby may well be Luke's way of underscoring that the holiness of the manger's humble occupant not only could not have been obvious to any observer, had it not been revealed to them by God, but even then could not be fully apprehended.

Call to Worship

Leader: Behold, I bring you good news of great joy!

People: FOR UNTO US IS BORN THIS DAY A SAVIOR AND A CHRIST!

Leader: Glory to God in the highest!

People: AND ON EARTH PEACE AND GOD'S GOOD WILL!

Collect

Great and glorious God, you have sent us a sign of our salvation hidden in the humility of a baby in a manger. Open our ears and our hearts to the good news of this event: that, like the shepherds of old, we may behold this thing that has come to pass, and praise and glorify you. In the name of the Christ-child we pray. Amen

Prayer of Confession

Most compassionate God, we sadly confess that we let the bustle and busy-ness of the Christmas season drown out the angelic message about the true meaning of this day, and lose sight of the sign of our salvation cradled in a crib. Forgive us, we pray, and let the angelic message ring again in our ears and drive us to behold as best we can, and to appreciate as much as we are able, the salvation that sleeps in a stable stall. In the name of the new-born Christ we pray. Amen

Christmas, Third Proper
(Christmas Eve/Day)

First Lesson: Isaiah 52:7-10

Theme: God's return to reign

Exegetical note: Deutero-Isaiah's enthronement announcement — "Your God reigns!" — and vision of Yahweh's return to Zion with salvation for all the world to see certainly were "good tidings of good" to a people demoralized by their captivity in Babylon. Verse 10, however, suggests that this good news is not restricted to that particular people or their historical situation, but is indeed universal and timeless.

Call to Worship
(based on Psalm 98)

Leader: Let all the earth make a joyful noise to God!

People: LET ALL ITS PEOPLE SING SONGS OF JOY!

Leader: For our God has not forgotten us!

People: OUR GOD HAS DONE A MARVELOUS THING!

Collect

God of majesty, you have always brought good tidings of redemption to people in every sort of captivity. Let your message of hope resound among us and within us: that, in the birth of the Christ, we may see the first light of the dawning of your blessed Reign and hear the marvelous news that will free us indeed. In his holy name we pray. Amen

Prayer of Confession

God of mercy, it is shameful how easily we accommodate ourselves to our captivity to the world and to the powers and principalities that govern it, and how consistently we forfeit the vision of your promised Reign, which alone can free us. Forgive us, O God, and let the coming of the Christ-child deepen our discontent with the world as it is, and heighten our hope for the world as it can be now that your divine grace and saving presence have come. In the name of Jesus we pray. Amen

Christmas, Third Proper
(Christmas Eve/Day)

Second Lesson: Hebrews 1:1-12

Theme: A comprehensive, cosmic Christ

Exegetical note: The author here begins his tight argument for the superiority of Christianity over Judaism by forging a Christology that has both Jewish Wisdom and Hellenistic elements. Though lacking any reference to Incarnation, the author speaks of the Christ in a protological ("through whom he created the world") and an eschatological ("the heir of all things") light, but depicts his real significance as being in the present, as the (1) reflection of God's nature and glory, (2) providential upholder of the cosmos, and (3) purifier of sins.

Call to Worship
(based on Psalm 98)

Leader: Let the sea roar, and everything in it!

People: LET THE WORLD SHOUT, AND ALL ITS PEOPLE!

Leader: Let the rivers and hills clap and sing!

People: FOR GOD COMES! HALLELUJAH!

Collect

Majestic and glorious God, you have sent us a child to be the Christ. Let the good news of his holy coming ring again in our hearts: that, despite the image of his humble birth, we may yet see his cosmic meaning as your creative, sustaining, and purifying agent of grace for this, our troubled world. In his magnificent name we pray. Amen

Prayer of Confession

Mighty and generous God, we humbly confess our limited imaginations when it comes to your workings, and especially with respect to your actions in Christ Jesus, whom we tend to view through our narrow vision and in light of our restricted desires. Forgive us, O God, and let the words of your holy Word remind us of the true magnitude of this Holy One, not only for us, our world, and our age, but for the infinities of time and space. In the name of the One who was, is, and is to be we pray. Amen

Christmas, Third Proper
(Christmas, Eve/Day)

Gospel: John 1:1-14

Theme: The creativity of the Christ

Exegetical note: In this quintessential protological (literally!) passage, the Christ is portrayed as the Incarnation ("enfleshment") of the Word (Logos) that, like the Jewish concept of Wisdom, was active in creation. But unlike Wisdom, which had been seen as the first creature, the Logos is here depicted as the uncreated, creative dynamic that was with God from the very beginning, and, presumably, active in history forever.

Call to Worship

Leader: In the beginning was the Word!

People: THE WORD WAS IN THE BEGINNING WITH GOD!

Leader: All things were made through the Word: for in the Word was life!

People: AND THAT WORD, WHO WAS LIFE, BECAME LIFE IN CHRIST! THANKS BE TO GOD!

Collect

Eternal God, you made your uncreated and creative Word to become one of us in order to bring us life and light. Prepare us to receive him anew: that, by the power of the Incarnation in Christ Jesus, we may be refashioned as new creatures in his likeness and your image. In his ageless name we pray. Amen

Prayer of Confession

Everliving and everloving God, we admit with dismay our penchant for reversing your miracle of incarnation, by remaking the Word, whom you made flesh in Christ Jesus, into some pure divinity who is only vaguely human rather than truly one of us. Forgive us, we pray, and help us to see and feel in him an actual person and true brother, in whom your divine and gracious presence nevertheless dwells, bringing us your life and light. In his sacred and saving name we pray. Amen

First Sunday after Chritmas
(Holy Family)

First Lesson: Isaiah 63:7-9

Theme: God's saving presence

Exegetical note: This passage is a typical introduction for a psalm of intercession in that it prefaces the lamentation and accompanying petition with a thanksgiving that recapitulates God's past saving acts. In this case the reference is to the Exodus and to God's "loving kindness" (or "steadfast love") and the "great goodness" that has come to Israel as a result. Notable here is the claim that they have been saved by "the angel of God's presence" (literally "face"), which is probably a reverential circumlocution for the immediate presence of Jahweh.

Call to Worship
(based on Psalm 111)

Leader: Give thanks to God with all your hearts!

People: GREAT ARE GOD'S WORKS, AND A PLEASURE TO BEHOLD!

Leader: Full of honor and majesty is everything God does!

People: AND THE RIGHTEOUSNESS OF GOD ENDURES FOREVER!

Collect

Steadfast God, you have always acted in loving kindness to redeem your people. Look kindly now upon us in this blessed season: that, sensing deeply the reality of your saving presence, we may know ourselves as members of your holy family — children of yours and sisters and brothers of Jesus. In his name we pray. Amen

Prayer of Confession

Savior God, we confess with dismay that we live much of our daily lives without any sense of your presence, as though everything that we do were completely in our hands and up to us, and that we live in much despair and disarray as a result. Forgive us, O God, and send us reminders that, whatever our human capacities and capabilities, it is only the power of your presence that finally saves and satisfies. In the precious name of Jesus the Christ we pray. Amen

First Sunday after Christmas
(Holy Family)

Second Lesson: Hebrews 2:10-18

Theme: Christ as our true brother

Exegetical note: Building upon the presupposition of the Christ's preexistence (1:1-4), the author here is at pains to assert the full humanity of this "pioneer" of salvation: he has the same origin as all his human siblings, he took the same "flesh and blood" nature as all God's children, and he is like them "in every respect," even in the experience of suffering and temptation.

Call to Worship

Leader: Brothers and sisters, let us proclaim God's name to one another!

People: LET US PRAISE GOD IN THE MIDST OF THIS CONGREGATION!

Leader: Let us trust God as a child trusts a mother or a father!

People: AND LET US GIVE THANKS TO GOD FOR THE SAVING GIFT OF OUR BROTHER, JESUS!

Collect

Most gracious God, you have been ever steadfast and dependable to your children. Help us to see in Christ Jesus a brother in every respect: that, sensing anew that we are members of your holy family, we may be drawn closer to one another as brothers and sisters, and to you as our loving and nurturing parent. In Jesus' name we pray. Amen

Prayer of Confession

God of love and mercy, it hurts to confess how little we members of your household have lived as true children of yours and brothers and sisters of Christ Jesus, and how often we have acted as though we were involved in a family feud. Forgive us, we pray, and give us an extra measure of your grace, so that we may learn to act with love and care toward one another in ways that will strengthen our family ties and extend our family circle. In the name of your Child and our Brother we pray. Amen

First Sunday after Christmas
(Holy Family)

Gospel: Matthew 2:13-15, 19-23

Theme: God's road to freedom

Exegetical note: Everything about this uniquely Matthewan account suggests that his purpose is not to recount actual history, but to depict Jesus as (1) the fulfillment of the Davidic-messianic expectations of the prophets, (2) Moses *redivivus*, and (3) the new Israel itself, called out of Egypt. In this context, the sojourn and eventual departure of the Holy Family for Galilee (under angelic orders!) suggest the beginning of a journey out of captivity and toward freedom.

Call to Worship
(based on Psalm 111)

Leader: The works of God's hands are faithful and just!

People: THE WORDS FROM GOD'S LIPS ARE TRUSTWORTHY AND TRUE!

Leader: God has sent redemption to a captive people!

People: GOD HAS ESTABLISHED A COVENANT WITH US FOREVER!

Collect

Provider God, you have time and again moved to free your people from every kind of captivity. Turn our attention to the journey of the Holy Family with the Christ-child out of Egypt: that, seeing there the first steps upon a path of liberating love, we may feel our lives released from all that enslaves us. In the name of the Christ we pray. Amen

Prayer of Confession

Protector God, we confess that we are in bondage in many areas of our lives, and have not yet either heard, or taken to heart your gracious call to liberation in Jesus. Forgive us, we pray, and coax and compel us out of our captivity. Lead us on your holy road toward the freedom and fulfillment, redemption and restoration, salvation and security that you have promised all your people. In the name of our pioneer and fellow traveler, Jesus, we pray. Amen

January 1
(When observed as Holy Name)

First Lesson: Numbers 6:22-27

Theme: The power of God's name

Exegetical note: The famous tripartite (so-called "Aaronic" or "Priestly") blessing in this passage is presented as a liturgical way to put God's name on Israel, which to the ancient mind meant to bestow upon them the full force of God's very being, saving presence, and sustaining providence.

Call to Worship
(based on Psalm 67)

Leader: May God's grace and blessing be upon us!

People: MAY GOD'S FACE SHINE UPON US!

Leader: May God's ways be known upon the earth!

People: MAY GOD'S SAVING POWER BE SEEN BY ALL NATIONS!

Collect

Gracious and blessed God, you have made your face to shine and your countenance to glow upon all the people of the earth. Help us who bear your name and the name of the Christ feel the power of those names: that, thus renewed by your mighty presence, we may find the strength to become redemptive forces in a weak and weary world. In the name of Jesus we pray. Amen

Prayer of Confession

Good and bountiful God, we confess that we take such pride in making names for ourselves, we seldom feel the force of your divine name, which we bear as Christians; and that we therefore live sad and sorry lives that may bring worldly recognition, but bear little heavenly fruit. Forgive us, we pray, and help us to tap the deep reserves of your holy power, so that we not only may strengthen ourselves, but may become channels of your divine energy to others. In the power of the name of Jesus we pray. Amen

January 1
(When observed as Holy Name)

Second Lesson: Philippians 2:9-13

Theme: The exalted name of Jesus

Exegetical note: It is not a terribly smooth transition from the final part of the Philippians hymn (vv. 9-11), which exalts Jesus' name, to the admonition to the reader (vv. 12-13) to work out her or his own salvation "with fear and trembling" and with a sense of God's being "at work" within. But the connective presupposition may well be the ancient belief that one's name entails one's very power and presence.

Call to Worship
(based on Psalm 67)

Leader: Let all the nations be glad and sing!

People: FOR GOD JUDGES THEIR PEOPLE WITH EQUITY!

Leader: Let all the peoples yield praise to God!

People: FOR GOD, OUR GOD, HAS BLESSED US!

Collect

Holy God, you have let the power and glory of your name be known by all the world's people. Now let us feel its presence and grace as well: that, moved by both your majesty and your mercy, we may realize and reflect your divine work and will in our lives, and may bear and share with others the name above every name, in which we pray. Amen

Prayer of Confession

Heavenly God, we are sad to confess that we take both your name and that of the Christ in vain, by failing to recognize what redemptive power those names have, and that we wear them as though mere labels or badges. Forgive us, we pray, and remind us of the awesome holy energy that is ours by virtue of your grace. Teach us to use that divine force for ourselves, and to direct it to others, so that all the world may know you and your desire to save. In the power of the name of Jesus we pray. Amen

January 1
(When observed as Holy Name)

Gospel: Luke 2:15-21

Theme: The power in the name of Jesus

Exegetical note: Luke's mention of the name Jesus (from the Aramaic Yeshua) here (with respect to the child's circumcision) and in 1:31 seems to recognize its importance by asserting that it was bestowed by an extraordinary agent (an angel); but in neither place is he as explicit as Matthew (1:21) about its meaning: "Yahweh saves." Other New Testament testimony makes it clear that by Luke's day, Christians venerated that name and regarded it as powerful, exalted, and salvific.

Call to Worship
(based on Psalm 67)

Leader: In the name of Jesus, let us worship God!

People: IN THE NAME OF JESUS, LET US SING AND PRAY!

Leader: In the name of Jesus, let us find release!

People: IN THE NAME OF JESUS, LET US TRUST AND HOPE!

Collect

Ageless God, you have sent us one whose very name means your presence and salvation. Inspire us now with his holy and heavenly power: that, beholding even the newborn Christ, we may see there your promise of redemption and our hope for salvation. In the name of Jesus, which assures us that "God saves," we trust and pray. Amen

Prayer of Confession

Almighty God, it grieves us to confess how lightly we take Jesus' name, how easily we affirm it, and how casually we wear it, forgetting the divine power and promise to save that is in it and the one who bore it. Forgive us, O God, and teach us to take it seriously, to affirm it boldly, and to wear it proudly as the hope, not only for ourselves, but for the world as well. In the mighty, exalted, redemptive, healing, precious name of Jesus, the Christ, we pray. **Amen**

Second Sunday after Christmas

First Lesson: Jeremiah 31:7-14

Theme: God's nurturing salvation

Exegetical note: This portion of a homecoming hymn, part of the so-called "Book of Consolation," looks to the return of Israel from Babylonian Exile ("the north country"). The line in verse 12 — "their life shall be like a watered garden" — provides a wonderful image for the salutary, nurturing effects of God's salvation upon the downtrodden and outcasts of every age.

Call to Worship
(based on Psalm 147)

Leader: Let us give thanks to God, who covers the heavens with clouds!

People: LET US GIVE THANKS TO GOD, WHO SENDS RAIN UPON THE EARTH!

Leader: Let us praise God, who makes grass to grow upon the hillsides!

People: LET US PRAISE GOD, WHO NURTURES AND SUSTAINS ALL CREATURES!

Collect

Holy and healing God, you have been the salvation of the captive and oppressed in every age. Help us to celebrate your redeeming work in Christ Jesus in this holy season: that, filled with the wonderful message that in him "God saves," we may gladly share with others that soothing gospel. In Jesus' name we pray. Amen

Prayer of Confession

Great and gracious God, we confess that we accommodate ourselves to the many kinds of captivity in which we find ourselves and our fellow humans, and fail to place our trust and hope in the healing promises of your gospel. Forgive us, we pray, and jolt us from our complacency by the power of your presence in the Christ. Make our lives like gardens, watered by your Holy Word and nourished by your Holy Spirit. In the name of the Christ we pray. Amen

Second Sunday after Christmas

Second Lesson: Ephesians 1:3-6, 15-18

Theme: God's accomplishment in Christ Jesus

Exegetical note: The termination of the second of these two fragments at verse 18 is unfortunate and misleading, giving the impression of a Gnostic petition. The whole passage (through verse 23), though admittedly a rambling syntactical jumble, needs to be taken into account so as to see the affirmation of Christ Jesus, not just as a conveyor of spiritual knowledge of salvation, but as the exalted one in whom God has accomplished that salvation.

Call to Worship
(based on Psalm 147)

Leader: It is good to sing praises to God!

People: FOR GOD IS GRACIOUS AND WORTHY OF OUR ADORATION!

Leader: God heals the brokenhearted and mends the wounded!

People: GOD GATHERS THE OUTCASTS AND LIFTS THE DOWNTRODDEN!

Collect

Life-giving God, you have sent us Christ Jesus, not just as a spiritual teacher or messenger of your grace and our salvation, but as the very one in whom your redemption is accomplished. Help us to receive him before this holy season has passed: that, full of awe and appreciation of your work in him, we may face the new year as new creatures. In his holy name we pray. Amen

Prayer of Confession

Most holy God, we confess that we do not fully comprehend the wonderful acts of yours that we have celebrated during this Christmas season; nor do we fully appropriate what little we do understand of your saving activity in Christ Jesus. Forgive us our hypocrisy, O God, and help us to take our own professions to heart, so that we may be at last doers of your Word, and not hearers and speakers only. In Jesus' name we pray. Amen

Second Sunday after Christmas

Gospel: John 1:1-18

Theme: God's eternal, creative Word

Exegetical note: It is not just the opening phrase of John's Prologue — "In the beginning" — that echoes the first verse of Genesis. Indeed the whole idea that the Word that is made flesh in Jesus is God's primeval creative agent, bringing both light and life, recalls the divine "fiats" of the Priestly author, whereby God, in effect, spoke the world into existence.

Call to Worship

Leader: Sisters and brothers, let us worship the God whose Word is Power!

People: LET US WORSHIP THE GOD WHOSE WORD IS MIGHT!

Leader: Let us worship the God whose Word is Life!

People: LET US WORSHIP THE GOD WHOSE WORD IS LIGHT!

Collect

Almighty Creator God, you spoke the universe to life and uttered light into the darkness with your eternal Word. Speak life and light into us as well: that, hearing again your voice in a Christ of our own flesh and blood, we may find ourselves the new creations that you would like us and have called us to be. In his holy name we pray. Amen

Prayer of Confession

God of amazing grace, we confess that we are not the new creations that you want us and have called us to be with your enlightening, enlivening Word. We live lives of darkness and death, and thereby mock your creative and redemptive power. Forgive us this blasphemy, O God, and speak again your life-giving, light-shedding Word-made-flesh in Christ. Then open our ears so that, hearing, we may be recreated in his image. In his name we pray. Amen

Epiphany

First Lesson: Isaiah 60:1-6

Theme: The magnetism of God's light

Exegetical note: This postexilic poem of Third Isaiah anticipates a time in which, because of God's arrival in glory, Jerusalem will be so radiant that all nations will be drawn to its light, bearing not only the children that have stayed behind in the land of captivity, but treasures, such as gold and frankincense. This passage, together with the responsorial Psalm 72, was apparently one of Matthew's sources for his story of the Magi.

Call to Worship
(based on Psalm 72)

Leader: Blessed is the God of Israel!

People: AND BLESSED IS THE ONE WHO COMES TO REIGN IN GOD'S NAME!

Leader: Before his spiritual majesty every earthly ruler will bow!

People: AND ALL NATIONS WILL SERVE HIM!

Collect

Most glorious God, you have sent us a Christ whose radiance puts to shame the glory of every earthly monarch. Let us be drawn again to his light: that, basking in his holiness and glory, we may be moved to a deeper love for you and for all your children. In the name of Christ Jesus we pray. Amen

Prayer of Confession

Most gracious God, we confess that we let ourselves be drawn to much that glitters and sparkles in the world, including luminous personalities and powerful people; and that we often pay more homage to them than to you and your Christ. Forgive us, O God, and draw our attention back to the majesty of the one who came in your name, bringing your earthly Reign, so that we shall return to you bearing our gifts and ourselves. In the name of Jesus we pray. Amen

Epiphany

Second Lesson: Ephesians 3:1-12

Theme: God's eternal plan: a Gospel for the world

Exegetical note: The axis around which this (probably pseudo-Pauline) passage turns is the idea of God's eternal and mysterious plan to extend the gospel of salvation in Christ to all humanity — a "mystery" apparently kept even from the heavenly host. This plan is now revealed by the Spirit to the apostles and prophets.

Call to Worship

Leader: Fellow sojourners, we meet to worship God!

People: OURS IS THE GOD OF ISRAEL, OF MOSES, OF DAVID!

Leader: But ours also is the God of the nations, the world, the universe!

People: LET US GIVE THANKS AND PRAISE TO THE ETERNAL GOD OF ALL!

Collect

God of everlasting love, you have graciously included all of humanity in your eternal plan of self-manifestation and salvation in Christ Jesus. Make us worthy recipients of its benefits by your grace: that, touched and tamed by your forgiveness, we may assist you in extending it to all the world. In Jesus' holy name we pray. Amen

Prayer of Confession

Most merciful God, we confess that our love and compassion are not as limitless as yours, and that we let our preferences and prejudices restrict the sharing of the gospel only to people who resemble ourselves. Forgive us, O God, and help us to overcome all of those affections and attitudes that stand in the way of our serving you and your eternal, divine plan to extend your love and care, your mercy and forgiveness in Jesus to all people. In his most holy name we pray. Amen

Jan 7, 1990

Epiphany

Gospel: Matthew 2:1-12

Theme: A Christ for all nations

Exegetical note: Matthew here artfully pieces together elements drawn from specific Old Testament texts (foreigners drawn to a divine light and bringing gold and frankincense from Isaiah 60:1-6; foreigners bearing gifts and paying tribute to a new king from Psalm 72; Bethlehem from Micah 5:2), in order to express the common belief that the salvation under the Messiah would apply to all nations. Later popular imagination went back to those source texts in order to turn the Magi into kings, name their kingdoms, and give them camels.

Call to Worship

Leader: And the wise men followed the star to its resting place.

People: AND WHEN THEY SAW THE CHILD THEY FELL DOWN AND WORSHIPED!

Leader: Then opening their treasures, they gave him gifts.

People: FOR THIS KING OF THE JEWS WAS THE REDEEMER OF ALL NATIONS!

Collect

Holy God of Israel, you have sent a Messiah bringing redemption, not just for his own people, but for all humankind. Let us behold him with those ancient visitors from the East: that, seeing his glory and recognizing his majesty, we may bow in wonder and depart to witness. in his holy name we pray. Amen

Prayer of Confession

Almighty God, we confess that we often lose any sense of awe before the Christ, and reduce him in our imaginations to the level of the commonplace and everyday. Forgive us, we pray, and impress upon us again his glory, his majesty, and his power as your savior of all humankind. Fill us with a sense of wonder and devotion to him and his holy mission as your Christ for our troubled world. In his high and holy name we pray. Amen

Baptism of our Lord
(First Sunday after the Epiphany)

First Lesson: Isaiah 42:1-9

Theme: A Servant with Spirit

Exegetical note: The identity of the Suffering Servant named in this so-called "First Servant Song" (vv. 1-4) is vague, referring either to Israel or to an anticipated individual. That this divinely-chosen servant was to be low-key and "a bruised reed," however, gave even the primitive Church reason to identify Jesus with the Servant; and God's declaration in v. 1 about placing the Spirit upon him and about his bringing "justice to the nations" certainly influenced the Synoptic accounts of Jesus' baptism.

Call to Worship
(based on Psalm 29)

Leader: The voice of God thunders upon the waters!

People: THE VOICE OF GOD IS FULL OF POWER AND MAJESTY!

Leader: The voice of God shakes the forest and the wilderness!

People: AND IN GOD'S TEMPLE ALL SHOUT, "GLORY!"

Collect

God of power and might, you sent us a Servant to be a Savior in the person of Christ Jesus. Help us to recall his baptism today: that, seeing there your Spirit descending upon him, we may realize his divine glory and your holy will to bring justice to a wicked and sinful world. In that Servant's holy name we pray. Amen

Prayer of Confession

God of peace and mercy, we confess that we rarely even notice the role of the Christ as a Suffering Servant of your divine will for world justice, probably because we fear in our hearts that we might have to swallow our pride and follow his way to the cross. Forgive us, we pray, and give us the courage and strength to leave our comfortable Christianity for a mission more in keeping with his teaching and example. In his name we pray. Amen

Baptism of our Lord
(First Sunday after the Epiphany)

Second Lesson: Acts 10:34-43

Theme: Jesus' baptism, God's epiphany

Exegetical note: Peter's kerygmatic reference to the baptism, like the accounts of Mark and John, treats that event as the inception of Jesus' ministry, for in it the Master receives the anointing of the Spirit that, in effect, makes him the Messiah-Christ (i.e., the "anointed One"). Notable throughout this passage is the fact that it is God who is the real agent, both at the baptism and in the entirety of Jesus' career.

Call to Worship
(based on Psalm 29)

Leader: God sits enthroned in royal majesty!

People: GOD RULES THE EARTH FOREVER!

Leader: May God give us strength!

People: MAY GOD BLESS US WITH PEACE!

Collect

Majestic God, you have sent us a Christ in whom and through whom you worked mighty acts for our salvation. Send now your Holy Spirit upon us: that, anointed and empowered as Jesus was at his baptism, we also may serve you in righteousness to the glory of your coming Reign and the honor of the one who established it. In his name we pray. Amen

Prayer of Confession

Merciful God, we confess that we continually make the mistake of trying to live and to minister "under our own steam," instead of opening ourselves to the working and direction of your Holy Spirit. Forgive us, we pray, and help us to take to heart the image of Jesus and to model ourselves after him, who accepted an anointing of water from John the Baptizer, and the anointing of the Spirit from you. In his name we pray. Amen

Baptism of our Lord
(First Sunday after the Epiphany)

Gospel: Matthew 3:13-17

Theme: An epiphany to the world

Exegetical note: Whereas Mark's earlier version of Jesus' baptism makes the theophany more subjective (with the voice from heaven addressing Jesus as a "Thou"), Matthew (with Luke) makes it more objective, with the divine declaration from above addressed to the bystanders. By making this personal event, in effect, public, Matthew may be declaring that this baptism was an epiphany to the world.

Call to Worship

Leader: Give thanks to the God of the Prophets!

People: GIVE PRAISE TO THE GOD OF THE BAPTIZER!

Leader: All glory to the God whose Spirit once descended on Jesus!

People: ALL HONOR TO THE GOD WHOSE HOLY PRESENCE INSPIRES US STILL!

Collect

O great God, you showered your Spirit upon Jesus and uttered words acknowledging him publicly as your own. Give us ears to hear and eyes to see your self-manifestation in that Holy One: that, moved by both your Word and mighty works in him, we may undertake ministry on behalf of you and your coming Reign. In the name of that anointed one we pray. Amen

Prayer of Confession

Gracious God, it saddens us to acknowledge how deaf and blind we often are to all of your self-manifestations in the world, and in particular to your unique self-disclosure in the life and ministry of Jesus. Forgive us, merciful God, and remove by the power of your Holy Spirit every internal and external obstacle to our recognizing in Jesus, his teachings, and his works the very presence and power of you. In his name we pray. Amen

Second Sunday after the Epiphany

First Lesson: Isaiah 49:1-7

Theme: Called from the womb for the world

Exegetical note: In this second Servant Song of Isaiah II, the Servant makes a public announcement of his divine, prenatal call directed to all nations. Noteworthy is the fact that after the prophet declares his inability to carry out his call, God not only repeats it, but expands it to include the "end of the earth," i.e., the entire world. The womb and the world here represent the bifocal nature of God's providence: the particular and the universal.

Call to Worship
(based on Psalm 40)

Leader: Let us tell the good news of deliverance!

People: LET US MAKE KNOWN THE SALVATION IN OUR HEARTS!

Leader: Let us proclaim God's faithfulness!

People: LET US DECLARE GOD'S STEADFAST LOVE!

Collect

Almighty God, your call to service is to particular individuals as well as to all humankind. Open our ears to your summoning voice: that, like the prophets of old before us, we may realize and claim in all humility the vocation that you have for us, both as individuals and as your earthly family. In the name of Jesus the Christ we pray. Amen

Prayer of Confession

All-merciful God, we confess with shame the many excuses we use to ignore your frequent and persistent callings for us to serve you, your Christ, and your coming Reign. Forgive us, we pray, and help us to put aside our alibis, our rationalizations, and our hardness of hearing and heart. Take us and make us effective despite our faults and fears, our liabilities and limitations, and our misgivings and mistakes. In the name of the One whose ministry and mission was heaven on earth we pray. Amen

Jan 14, 1990

Second Sunday after the Epiphany

Second Lesson: 1 Corinthians 1:1-9

Theme: Sainthood in solidarity

Exegetical note: Paul's typically "Christianized" version of the standard ancient epistle greeting here (vv. 1-3) revolves around two focal ideas: "call" and "church." His own call is specific: to be an apostle. Their call is more general, but yet universal in scope: to be saints, not just in their local church, but in solidarity with all who everywhere profess Christ.

Call to Worship
(based on Psalm 40)

Leader: May those who seek God rejoice!

People: MAY THOSE WHO LOVE SALVATION BE GLAD!

Leader: God is our deliverer and our help!

People: GOD IS OUR PRESERVER AND OUR HOPE!

Collect

O Holy God, you have called us to a holiness that is not just individual and personal, but corporate and universal in scope. Expand our vision: that, beholding at last the solidarity of our saintly fellowship, we may see ourselves in terms of your desire to bring salvation, not just to ourselves, but to our world. In the name of the Christ we pray. Amen

Prayer of Confession

God of humankind, we confess that we are extremely selfish in all things, and even in the ways in which we interpret your salvation. We gladly claim it for ourselves and bask in its promises, but then act as though we were a Christ-clique. Forgive us, we pray. Overcome our self-centeredness with Christ-centeredness, so that his love and concern, compassion and care for all the world's people may become ours by your grace. In his holy and universal name we pray. Amen

Second Sunday after the Epiphany

Gospel: John 1:29-34

Theme: Witnessing God's Word

Exegetical note: John's version of Jesus' baptism is, at best, inferential, but the witness of the Baptizer to Jesus is direct and unambiguous, the result of both visual and aural evidence: he sees the Spirit descend "like a dove" and rest upon Jesus; and he hears the very voice of God. The Baptizer's (as well as the Evangelist's!) testimony, therefore, is unequivocal: "this is the Son of God" and "the Lamb of God who takes away the world's sin."

Call to Worship

Leader: Behold the Child of God!

People: WHO BAPTIZES WITH GOD'S SPIRIT!

Leader: Behold the Lamb of God,

People: WHO TAKES AWAY THE WORLD'S SIN!

Collect

Glorious God, you have given us a wonderful and redemptive gift in the person of Jesus. Teach us to bear witness to him: that, like the Baptizer of old, we may deliver to all who will hear a testimony of unequivocal and unambiguous certainty, so effective and compelling that others will be unable to ignore or resist him. In his name we pray. Amen

Prayer of Confession

Gracious God, it grieves us to confess how timid and tentative our testimony to Jesus really has been, and how ineffective and unconvincing our witness generally is as a result. Forgive us, we pray, and fill us with the deepest faith and conviction by the power of your Spirit, so that our hearts will overflow with love and our words and our works will declare that Jesus is the Christ, the very Lamb of God, who takes away the sins of the world. In his redeeming name we pray. Amen

Third Sunday after the Epiphany

First Lesson: Isaiah 9:1-4

Theme: God's glory for Galilee's gloom

Exegetical note: First Isaiah, writing in the context of the Assyrian conquest of Galilee, nevertheless speaks confidently of God's glorious restoration. In doing so, he equates the current captivity with the darkness of night and the anticipated liberation with the light of day. As a reading after the Epiphany, the passage's parallel with the beginning of Jesus' ministry in Galilee is striking.

Call to Worship
(based on Psalm 27)

Leader: God is our light and our salvation!

People: WHOM SHALL WE FEAR?

Leader: God is the refuge of our lives!

People: WHY SHOULD WE BE AFRAID?

Collect

Most glorious God, you brought your radiant light to brighten our sin-darkened world in the person of Jesus. Let his brilliance shine upon us again this day: that, our lives divinely illuminated by his wonderful presence, we may find our gloom raised to glory and our darkness turned to dawn. In his most holy name we pray. Amen

Prayer of Confession

Most gracious God, we admit with great humility that we often wallow in the very darkness of sin that you sent Jesus to dispel, and sometimes even try to block the brilliance of your grace when it threatens to break through and shed light on our wicked ways. Forgive us, O God, and weaken our resistance, so that our wills may finally become transparent to and reflective of the brightness of his holy face and the illumination of your glorious grace. In Jesus' name we pray. Amen

Third Sunday after the Epiphany

Second Lesson: 1 Corinthians 1:10-17

Theme: Community in the Christ

Exegetical note: Having received reports that the Corinthian congregation has been torn by dissension, the Apostle writes from Ephesus to call for unity of mind over against party allegiances based on particular luminaries (himself included!), and probably on their personalities more than their teachings at that. The heart of Paul's appeal is for community in the Christ, who alone was crucified for them, and in whom alone they were baptized.

Call to Worship

Leader: Grace to all who are sanctified in Christ Jesus!

People: GRACE TO ALL WHO ARE CALLED TO BE SAINTS TOGETHER!

Leader: Peace to all who everywhere call upon the name of Jesus!

People: PEACE FROM GOD AND THE CHRIST OF ALL!

Collect

God of binding love, you have given us one Christ, one faith, and one baptism in which to find community with you and one another. Lead us to a sense and spirit of true Christian unity: that, seeing beyond our affiliations and allegiances to this church or that denomination, we may find our real identity as members of the body of the Christ, in whose name we pray. Amen

Prayer of Confession

God of infinite mercy, we admit that we love dissension more than we should, and that we make and multiply divisions within the Church, and align ourselves with particular spiritual leaders, and all the while further the brokenness of the body of Christ. Forgive us, we pray, and teach us to look beyond the religious labels of our own devising, in order to see the community that befits a people who call themselves Christians. Make us the Church, one in the Spirit and one in the Christ, loyal to no one but him and you. In his holy name we pray. Amen

Jan 21, 1990

Third Sunday after the Epiphany

Gospel: Matthew 4:12-23

Theme: Calling for repentance for a Reign that is coming

Exegetical note: Matthew's rendition of the beginning of Jesus' ministry agrees with the other Synoptic Gospels in identifying Galilee as the point of departure. But his distinctive connection with "the Galilee of the Gentiles" of Isaiah 9:1-2 is probably intended to underscore the universality of Jesus' mission, of which Matthew here offers a compendium: preaching the nearness of the coming Reign of God ("heaven" is a circumlocution), calling upon all to repent and some to follow, and healing.

Call to Worship

Leader: Rejoice! For once we sat in darkness!

People: BUT NOW WE HAVE SEEN A GREAT LIGHT!

Leader: Give thanks! For all humanity once languished in the shadow of death!

People: BUT NOW THE LIGHT HAS DAWNED!

Collect

Provident God, you sent Jesus to announce and activate your coming heavenly and holy Reign upon earth. Make his ministry and mission come alive again for us: that, seeing your very presence in his every act and hearing your very word in his every saying, we may learn to live for that glorious day when your Holy Rule will be total. In his name we pray. Amen

Prayer of Confession

Precious God, we confess that we lose both sight and sense of the nearness of your Holy Rule, which Jesus came preaching with parables and witnessing with wonders, and that we live instead in our own world with our own rules, with little or no concern about whether your will is done on earth or not. Forgive us, we pray, and by your Holy Spirit turn our attention to your dawning Reign and our affection to your Christ, so that all of the benefits of your love, grace and forgiveness may be ours. Amen

Fourth Sunday after the Epiphany

First Lesson: Micah 6:1-8

Theme: The requirements of God

Exegetical note: Prophesying at the end of the eighth century B.C. in the southern kingdom of Judah, Micah ignores such international and political incidents as the invasion of the Assyrians and concentrates instead on social injustices. Here God has a "controversy" with the Israelites and intends to "contend" with them and require of them — in the spirit of Amos, Hosea, and Isaiah — not ritual sacrifice, but justice, loving kindness, and a humble walking with God.

Call to Worship

Leader: With what shall we come and bow before God?

People: NOT WITH BURNT OFFERINGS! NOT WITH RIVERS OF OIL! NOT WITH THE FRUITS OF OUR LABORS!

Leader: What has God shown us? What does God require?

People: THAT WE DO JUSTICE! THAT WE LOVE KINDNESS! THAT WE WALK HUMBLY WITH GOD!

Collect

God of Israel Old and New, you have set before us in scripture clear requirements for service to you. Help us to read and heed the words of your will: that, moved to true godliness, we may live lives of justice and loving kindness, and thus walk always in humility with you. In Jesus' name we pray. Amen

Prayer of Confession

God of eternal promise, we confess with the deepest regret that we have not lived with justice and loving kindness in mind, but have instead devoted and dedicated ourselves to self-serving ends and selfish goals, mindless of the injustices and suffering we were bringing to others and to the earth itself. Forgive us, O God, and let the words of your ancient prophets lead us to your true righteousness, which is justice, and your authentic holiness, which is compassion. In the Christ's holy name we pray. Amen

Fourth Sunday after the Epiphany

Second Lesson: 1 Corinthians 1:18-31

Theme: Our foolish wisdom, God's wise folly

Exegetical note: Against the Corinthians' inclination toward esoteric knowledge and the spiritual self-satisfaction that it engendered, Paul here asserts that the Christian gospel of salvation is foolishness in comparison with worldly wisdom; that the wisdom that is so valued by Greeks is as ineffectual as the signs demanded by Jews; and that God purposely chose the foolish and the weak to shame the wise and the strong, so that the "boast" of all might be God and not themselves and their achievements.

Call to Worship
(based on Psalm 37)

Leader: Let us take delight in God!

People: LET US COMMIT OURSELVES TO GOD'S WAYS!

Leader: Let us be still before God!

People: LET US WAIT PATIENTLY BEFORE GOD!

Collect

God of all wisdom, you have scorned our best wisdom and knowledge and have commended to us instead the foolishness of a divine Word made flesh and manifested in humility. Transform our values, O God, and teach us to put our trust in your inconceivable grace rather than the works of our imaginations. In the name of your Redeeming One we pray. Amen

Prayer of Confession

God of all grace, it shames us to admit how arrogant we have been about our own minds, intellects, knowledge and wisdom, as though these would bring our ultimate salvation and triumph over troubles and sufferings. In fact, they have led us to pollute the earth and to mine from her the instruments of oppression and annihilation. Forgive us our self-satisfaction, we pray, and turn our thoughts and hopes upon you and your precious grace, however foolish it appears to the eyes of this world. In Jesus' name we pray. Amen

Fourth Sunday after the Epiphany

Gospel: Matthew 5:1-12

Theme: Bleak realities, but blessed rewards

Exegetical note: Matthew's location of Jesus' great Sermon on the Mount is undoubtedly meant to strike a parallel with Moses and the Old Law. Here Jesus begins with the Beatitudes, which are addressed, not to a general audience, but to those — apparently the lowliest and most oppressed of society — who have devoted themselves to the inbreaking Reign. For them, the bleak realities of the present will give way to the blessed rewards of God's future.

Call to Worship

Leader: Blessed is the God of Israel!

People: BLESSED IS THE GOD OF JESUS!

Leader: Blessed are we who await God's Reign!

People: BLESSED ARE ALL WHOSE GLOOMY REALITIES WILL BECOME GLORIOUS REWARDS!

Collect

Sovereign God, you have set before us the promise, not of worldly wealth, but of royal riches in your coming Reign. Help us to alter our ambitions and to adjust our aims: that, no longer seduced by the thrill of acquiring and procuring, possessing and accumulating the things of this world, we may set our sights on the true treasures of your spiritual realms. In Jesus' name we pray. Amen

Prayer of Confession

Longsuffering God, we humbly confess that we have sold our souls to become the very rich against whom Jesus pronounced "woes," and have ignored and even increased the sufferings of the lowly and oppressed whom Jesus called "blessed." Forgive us our ungodly values, we pray, and give us the grace to forsake the images of success that inspire the world, and to claim as our status symbol your Suffering Servant. In his name we pray. Amen

Fifth Sunday after the Epiphany

First Lesson: Isaiah 58:3-9a

Theme: Ritual versus righteousness

Exegetical note: Trito-Isaiah, writing in the context of the early days of the return of the exiles from Babylon, expresses here the consternation of the people whose supplicatory fasting has had no effect, and delivers a scathing divine rejection of such routine ritual in favor of the acts of human liberation that God does find acceptable: freeing the oppressed, feeding the hungry, housing the homeless, clothing the naked. For such righteous activity will bring the healing of God's presence.

Call to Worship
(based on Psalm 112)

Leader: Blessed are those who are generous!

People: BLESSED ARE THOSE WHO ARE JUST!

Leader: For it is they who firmly trust God!

People: IT IS THEY WHOSE HEARTS ARE STEADFAST!

Collect

Most royal God, you have taught us again and again that the true worship of you is the doing of justice, and that real service to you is the living of compassion. Set this truth again upon our hearts: that, inspired by the words of your prophets and the example of your Christ, we may trade our religiousness for your righteousness. In Jesus' name we pray. Amen

Prayer of Confession

Most righteous God, we humbly confess that, despite your many warnings, we have placed most of our spiritual energies into religion that would lead to individual salvation rather than into righteousness that would establish your Reign of justice for all. Forgive us our selfishness, O God, and help us to dedicate ourselves, not to self-satisfying ceremony, but to sacrificial service on behalf of your Christ and the blessed ones of his Reign. In his name we pray. Amen

Fifth Sunday after the Epiphany

Second Lesson: 1 Corinthians 2:1-11

Theme: Wisdom received versus wisdom achieved

Exegetical note: Among the most popular and revered individuals in Paul's day were the professional, itinerant orators, skilled and educated in rhetoric, who could extemporize on virtually any topic, and mesmerize less with substance than with style. With these Paul contrasts himself, who has only a haltingly-delivered, simple message for the many — "Christ and him crucified" — and wisdom for "the mature." Yet even that is not the achieved wisdom of the learned, but the received wisdom revealed by the Spirit of God.

Call to Worship
(based on Psalm 112)

Leader: Praise God, who is gracious!

People: PRAISE GOD, WHO IS RIGHTEOUS!

Leader: Praise God, who is merciful!

People: PRAISE GOD, WHO BRINGS LIGHT TO THE DARKNESS FOR THE UPRIGHT!

Collect

Eternal God, you have taught us repreatedly that our hope is not in the spiritual knowledge that we achieve for ourselves, or the insights that we accept from pious professionals, but in the wisdom we receive from you in Christ Jesus. Remind us again of that great truth: that, trusting at last in the Word of Wisdom that alone is effective, we may find real righteousness and perfect peace. In Jesus' name we pray. Amen

Prayer of Confession

Most loving God, it pains us to confess how easily we have been seduced by slick-tongued purveyors of purported spirituality, and how willingly we have followed any path that they promised would solve our problems and make our lives meaningful and happy. Forgive us our gullibility, O God, and point us again to the true but subtle wisdom of your gospel in Jesus, in which alone is our hope and our salvation. In his holy name we pray. Amen

Fifth Sunday after the Epiphany

Gospel: Matthew 5:13-16

Theme: Enlightened discipleship

Exegetical note: In an odd combination (though not quite a mixture) of metaphors, Matthew here has Jesus refer to his disciples as "salt" and "light" with respect to their role in bringing salvation to the world. The more developed of the two images is the latter: the disciples' "light," which is to be flaunted rather than obscured, is apparently their good works, which in turn reflect, not the efforts or inherent righteousness of the doers, but the glory of a gracious God.

Call to Worship

Leader: Let us worship the God of Light!

People: LET US PRAISE THE LIGHT OF THE WORLD!

Leader: Let us make our own lights to shine through all the earth!

People: TO THE GLORY AND HONOR OF GOD AND CHRIST JESUS!

Collect

God of Light, you have called us to ministries of illumination in a sin-darkened world. Make us reflective of the spiritual radiance of the Christ: that, aglow with the redemption that only he radiates, we may shed his Light around us in ways that brighten the world and all its inhabitants. In the his name we pray. Amen

Prayer of Confession

God of love, we humbly confess that we do not always reflect the radiance of your precious Christ, and that we sometimes even contribute in many unfortunate ways to the darkness of sin that enshrouds the world to its detriment and damnation. Forgive us, we pray, and let our lights so shine that others may see in their glow your holy and healing Light, and may find thereby the Way that leads to life and peace. In Jesus' holy name we pray. Amen

Sixth Sunday after the Epiphany

First Lesson: Deuteronomy 30:15-20

Theme: Choosing life by loving God

Exegetical note: the blessing and curse (vv. 16-18) and the invoking of witnesses (v. 19) are standard parts of ancient near-Eastern covenants, of which Deuteronomy 19-20 is a good example. The covenant in question here is not the Sinaitic one, but one initiated at Moab (perhaps a renewal of the earlier one) just before the Israelites entered into the promised land. The choice offered is clear-cut (life and blessing versus death and evil) and immediate ("today"), and hinges on obedience to and love of God.

Call to Worship
(based on Psalm 119)

Leader: Blessed are those whose ways are pure!

People: BLESSED ARE THOSE WHO WALK IN GOD'S WAYS!

Leader: Blessed are those who keep God's commands!

People: BLESSED ARE THOSE WHO TRULY LOVE GOD!

Collect

God of Original Blessing, you filled the universe with your creative energy when you called it forth from nothingness and declared it good. Help us to find our proper place in your created order: that, seeing ourselves in oneness with all your creatures, we may yet exhibit the image and likeness of yourself in which you made us. In Jesus' name we pray. Amen

Prayer of Confession

God of Eternal Life, we confess that we have not always chosen the life and blessedness that you have offered us as the natural reward for obedience and service to you, but instead have fallen into ways of life that promote sin and death. Forgive us, we pray, and turn our attention upon your self-manifestation in Christ Jesus, who alone of all your creatures was transparent to your gracious presence in the universe. In his holy name we pray. Amen

Sixth Sunday after the Epiphany

Second Lesson: 1 Corinthians 3:1-9

Theme: Misplaced affections

Exegetical note: Paul continues to concern himself with the party loyalties that have arisen at Corinth, and perhaps the charge that his teachings have been too simplistic, especially as compared to the professional rhetoricians who abounded and appealed to the affections of the "mere mortals" who were "still of the flesh." In the process he now wishes to relativize both himself and his chief rival Apollos, on the grounds that it is really God who deserves the credit for the growth of (presumably) the gospel.

Call to Worship
(based on Psalm 119)

Leader: Let us praise God with upright hearts!

People: LET US KEEP OUR WAYS PURE!

Leader: Let us seek God with our whole hearts!

People: LET US GUIDE OUR PATHS ACCORDING TO GOD'S WORD!

Collect

Nurturing God, you have provided us with the potential and means for spiritual growth. Teach us to look only to you and your gifts for the nourishment we need: that, trusting in your creative Spirit rather than any worldly allegiance, we may truly become the holy people that you would have us to be. In Jesus' name we pray. Amen

Prayer of Confession

God of infinite compassion, we confess that we often fall into the trap of following the attractive utterances of persuasive teachers and preachers, and wind up devoting ourselves to them rather than to you and your gospel. Forgive us for being so fickle, O God, and draw us like a magnet back to your saving truth in Christ Jesus, which surpasses all wordly wisdom and human understanding. In his holy name we pray. Amen

Sixth Sunday after the Epiphany

Gospel: Matthew 5:17-26

Theme: The inner demands of God's Law

Exegetical note: Here begins the section of Matthew's version of the Sermon on the Mount that contains the so-called "antitheses" of Jesus concerning the Law. Having asserted that he has come to fulfill rather than abolish the Law and the prophets, Jesus proceeds to quote the Law ("You have heard it said...") and then to intensify it ("But I say...") by extending its purview to cover inner motivation. The first antithesis, contained in this passage, is typical in that it moves beyond the act of murder to the feelings that lead to it.

Call to Worship

Leader: Sisters and brothers, we meet to worship a loving God!

People: WE MEET TO WORSHIP A GOD WITH HIGH STANDARDS!

Leader: We meet in the name of a God who knows our deepest hearts!

People: WE MEET IN THE PRESENCE OF A GOD WHO LOVES US ANYWAY!

Collect

Ageless God, you gave us first a covenant of Law and later a testament of grace so that we might live in reconciliation and harmony with you. Turn us from futile rule-following and commandment-keeping: that, focusing within, we may find our true peace, not in religious activities, but in righteous affections. In Jesus' name we pray. Amen

Prayer of Confession

Almighty God, we confess that we are often more interested in trying to fulfill the letter of your holy Law than in living according to its spirit, and that we wind up failing miserably to do either. Forgive us, we pray, and inspire us with the teachings and example of the Christ, who taught us that if we attend to our inner righteousness by entrusting it to your grace, works of goodness and righteousness will surely follow. In his spirit and name we pray. Amen

Seventh Sunday after the Epiphany

First Lesson: Isaiah 49:8-13

Theme: God's compassion for the captive

Exegetical note: Following the Second Servant Song (vv. 1-6 or 1-7), this poetic passage announces confidently (though no doubt proleptically) God's compassion and comfort for an afflicted people as a *fait accompli* in "a time of favor" and "a day of salvation." The obvious allusion is to the Exodus, the perennial model for God's redemptive activity on behalf of all who are captive to any sort of enslavement.

Call to Worship
(based on Psalm 62)

Leader: For God alone do our souls wait in silence!

People: GOD ALONE IS OUR HOPE!

Leader: God alone is our rock and our salvation!

People: GOD ALONE IS OUR FORTRESS, AND WE SHALL NOT BE SHAKEN!

Collect

God of constant love, you have always brought release to those in every sort of captivity. Help us to hear your message of liberation in this day and time: that, filled with the good news of your freeing grace, we may shake off the bonds and shackles of all that enslaves us, and live as free people redeemed in Christ Jesus. In his name we meet and pray. Amen

Prayer of Confession

God of liberating compassion, we confess that we often feel ourselves hopelessly bound to limiting forces within and without, and that we succumb to these all too readily and willingly. Forgive us, we pray, and move us again with the freeing power of your will and your word. Help us to fight off addictions, compulsions, habits, restrictions, and limitations, and to move gracefully toward becoming all that we can be by the power of your Spirit. In Jesus' name we pray. Amen

Seventh Sunday after the Epiphany

Second Lesson: 1 Corinthians 3:10-11, 16-23

Theme: Divisiveness as defilement

Exegetical note: Still addressing the issue of fractious party loyalties at Corinth, Paul here uses temple imagery for the Church. The passage provides a special opportunity for emphasizing that the Church is not for Paul a building or organization, as it generally is for twentieth-century readers, but people. When understood as pure imagery, however, the building motif does work well in treating ecclesiastical divisiveness as the equivalent of ritual defilement.

Call to Worship
(based on Psalm 62)

Leader: Let us trust in God always!

People: LET US POUR OUT OUR HEARTS BEFORE GOD!

Leader: God is our rock!

People: GOD IS OUR REFUGE!

Collect

God of history, you have always commended love to us not only as a bond between us and you, but as a source of community among ourselves as well. Fill this church with the unitive power of your Spirit: that, drawn together by your healing power, we may feel among ourselves and exhibit to others the harmony that should prevail in all of human society. In Jesus' name we pray. Amen

Prayer of Confession

God of harmony, it grieves us to admit how often we have sown and spread, tolerated and transmitted disunity and divisiveness both within the church and without, thus disgracing your gospel of love and peace. Forgive us, we pray, and fill us with your Spirit of holiness and wholeness. Heal all wounds and mend all fractures that keep us from being the Christian Church and human family that you would have us to be. In the Christ's name we pray. Amen

Seventh Sunday after the Epiphany

Gospel: Matthew 5:27-37

Theme: Jesus' "higher righteousness"

Exegetical note: These verses contain three of the so-called "antitheses" of Jesus' Sermon on the Mount, in which he intensifies the demands of the Law. Here, lust is equated with adultery, divorce is forbidden (the exception being Matthew's, not Jesus'), and swearing (as opposed to merely false swearing) is prohibited. In each case, Jesus is calling for a "higher righteousness" that moves beyond external obedience to a moral code, to an internal orientation toward God's will.

Call to Worship

Leader: Brothers and sisters, let us worship God!

People: LET US WORSHIP IN WORD AND IN SONG!

Leader: Let us worship in praise and in prayer!

People: LET US WORSHIP IN SPIRIT AND IN TRUTH!

Collect

Eternal God, you have given us an Old Covenant as a measure of your expectation, and a New Testament as an indication of your affection. Help us to turn our attention within: that, seeing the futility of fulfilling the letter of the Law of Moses, we may be thrown back upon the goodness of your grace in Jesus. In his name we pray. Amen

Prayer of Confession

Merciful God, we confess that despite your many warnings, we still try to be righteous either by doing good or by not doing bad, and that we fail miserably at both. Forgive us, we pray, and teach us at last to trust in the sufficiency of your grace rather than our own efforts. Transform us from within by the power of your Spirit, and let the good works follow as the fruits of your divine action and evidence of the higher righteousness that is ours in Christ Jesus, in whose name we pray. Amen

Eighth Sunday after the Epiphany

First Lesson: Leviticus 19:1-2, 9-18

Theme: Public holiness

Exegetical note: The first two verses of this chapter set the theme: holiness. Two things about the holiness commended here to the Israelites are noteworthy: (1) it is derivative from God's, not generated by the people; (2) it is a public holiness (as opposed to a private inner state of the soul) expressed in visible deeds. This public holiness is mostly directed toward the "neighbor" (i.e., the fellow Israelite), but is also active on behalf of the sojourning stranger (vv. 10 and 33).

Call to Worship
(based on Psalm 119)

Leader: The ways of God are paths to rightousness!

People: LET US TURN OUR MINDS TOWARD GOD'S COMMANDMENTS!

Leader: In the righteousness of God are life and hope!

People: LET US TURN OUR HEARTS TO THE KEEPING OF GOD'S LAWS!

Collect

Most holy God, you have reminded us again and again that whatever holiness we have is not of our own doing, but the result of the overflowing of your own bounteous righteousness. Confer upon us your gracious goodness: that, thus endowed, we may cultivate lives of justice and peace in our troubled world. In the name of Jesus we pray. Amen

Prayer of Confession

God of heaven and earth, we confess with regret that we often take holiness as a private matter of the inner soul rather than a public ministry of justice for our fellow human beings. Forgive us our shortsighted selfishness, O God, and give us a measure of your boundless compassion. Set before us as an example the life of Jesus, the Christ, whose holiness meant wholeness for all in need. In his precious name we pray. Amen

Eighth Sunday after the Epiphany

Second Lesson: 1 Corinthians 4:1-5

Theme: Servant-stewards vs. status seekers

Exegetical note: Still in the background of Paul's thoughts here is the problem of party-loyalties that he raised in the first chapter. Now he asserts that true spiritual leaders are to be servants and stewards of "God's mysteries" (which for Paul means the gospel itself) — presumably rather than popular luminaries or status-seekers — and that they are to be judged, not by present human standards, but eschatologically by God.

Call to Worship

Leader: Sisters and brothers, we gather to celebrate the mysteries of God!

People: WE MEET TO SHARE THE GOSPEL OF JESUS CHRIST!

Leader: May all we do be to God's liking!

People: MAY ALL WE SAY BE TO GOD'S GLORY!

Collect

Exalted God, you have called us to be stewards of your gospel and servants to our fellow human beings in your name. Fill us with your abiding presence: that, empowered by your divine energy, we may fulfill those holy roles rather than ones of our own devising. In the name of Jesus we pray. Amen

Prayer of Confession

Enabler God, we confess the awful extent to which we spend our precious time seeking status in the eyes of the world and pursuing power on the world's terms rather than striving to be servants and stewards of your Reign. Forgive us our foolish selfishness, O God, and empower us with your Holy Spirit to become what you would have us to be and to do what you would have us to do. In the name of your Christ, our brother, we pray. Amen

Eighth Sunday after the Epiphany

Gospel: Matthew 5:38-48

Theme: Emulating God's love

Exegetical note: These last two of Jesus's so-called antitheses ("You have heard it said..., but I say...") continue Jesus' radicalization of the righteousness of (in the first instance) the Old Testament statutes and (in the second) conventional wisdom. The closing demand for perfection (v. 48) should not be taken literally or our of context, but in light of vv. 43ff., as an exhortation to emulate God's perfect love, which, like the sunshine and the rain, benefits even the evil and the unjust.

Call to Worship

Leader: Let us worship the God of Creation!

People: LET US WORSHIP THE GOD OF LOVE!

Leader: May God's blessings be upon us this day!

People: MAY GOD'S LOVE — AND OURS — FLOW TO ALL PEOPLE!

Collect

God of absolute justice, you have called us to imitate your own righteousness in our dealings with one another. Help us again to hear and heed that vocation: that, laying aside our selfish motives and self-serving ways, we may become truly worthy citizens of your coming Reign in Christ Jesus, in whose name we pray. Amen

Prayer of Confession

God of perfect love, we confess that we fail regularly and miserably to emulate your righteous love as Jesus taught us to in word and deed, but instead pursue private and comfortable forms of personal piety that only make us look good and feel holy. Forgive us, O God, and set before us the Christ. Help us through your gracious power to conform ourselves to your standards and his example, and thus to become responsible and productive citizens of your Holy Realm. In Jesus' name we pray. Amen

Feb 25, 90

Last Sunday after the Epiphany
(The Transfiguration of Our Lord)

First Lesson: Exodus 24:12-18

Theme: The hidden majesty of God

Exegetical note: The fact that in this theophany on the mountain Moses beholds, not God, but God's glory reflects the recurring Old Testament belief that to behold the "face" of the Deity is unbearable and potentially fatal. The images of cloud and fire for God's presence are a recurring motif of the Priestly writer (cf. the two "pillars" in 13:21-22), again signifying that although God is always present, that presence is veiled and mysterious due to the awesome majesty of the Holy One.

Call to Worship

Leader: May the glory of the God of Israel surround us!

People: MAY THE MAJESTY OF THE GOD OF ALL NATIONS INSPIRE US!

Leader: May the presence of the God of Moses be with us!

People: MAY THE GRACE OF THE GOD OF JESUS BE UPON US!

Collect

God of hidden majesty, you have revealed yourself to humanity in many ways, both public and private. Sensitize us to all of your manifestations: that, filled with a sense of your presence, we may draw on your power and strength and move to new heights of holiness and righteousness as servants of you and the Christ. In his holy name we pray. Amen

Prayer of Confession

God of manifest mercy, it is difficult but necessary for us to admit how closed our eyes, hearts, and minds are to your presence in the world, and how much we live, for all intents and purposes, as godless and unspiritual people. Forgive us our insensitivity, we pray, and keep us aware of your being with us. Make us living embodiments and evidence of your abiding and active care for your creation and all of its creatures, even as Jesus was. In his name and spirit we pray. Amen

Last Sunday after the Epiphany
(The Transfiguration of Our Lord)

Second Lesson: 2 Peter 1:16-21

Theme: God's incarnate Light

Exegetical note: Since the Second Coming of Jesus is a central concern of this very late pseudonymous epistle, that is almost certainly the meaning of the coming *(parousia)* of Jesus mentioned in v. 16. The account of the transfiguration of Jesus here is intended to affirm the historicity of the gospel as well as to confirm the authority of the writer, as a witness to that/the first Christophany, to make pronouncements about the second. The light imagery ("lamp," "star," "dawn") that he uses in the process is typical of biblical theophanies, but nonetheless moving.

Call to Worship

Leader: We meet in the name of the Light of the world!

People: WE MEET IN THE NAME OF THE INCARNATE CHRIST!

Leader: May the power of God's presence be with us!

People: MAY THE LIGHT OF GOD'S GLORY BE UPON US!

Collect

Most brilliant God, you have called us to let our lights shine on behalf of you, your Christ, and your coming Reign. Set our souls aglow with your Spirit: that, thus illumined from within, we may radiate the perfect love of the one true Light, in whose name we pray. Amen

Prayer of Confession

Merciful God, we humbly confess that, rather than being instruments of your divine Light that drive out spiritual darkness, we often live as though victims of that darkness whose souls are, at best, dim candles. Forgive us our failure to reflect the brightness of your love and mercy, O God, and make us radiant lamps for your coming Reign until its bright day at last dawns in all its glory. In Jesus' name we pray. Amen

Last Sunday after the Epiphany
(The Transfiguration of Our Lord)

Gospel: Matthew 17:1-9

Theme: The One who radiates God

Exegetical note: The idea of God's presence being signified by a cloud (albeit a bright one!) has much Old Testament precedent (e.g., Exodus 24:15-18), and here provides a marvelous contrast with the sun-like radiance of Jesus. It is noteworthy that the disciples here cannot bear either the sight or the sound of the awesome "enclouded" God (v. 6) but the God whom Jesus radiates (versus reflects) they may behold directly (v. 8).

Call to Worship

Leader: Jesus Christ is the Light of the world!

People: JESUS CHRIST IS THE MANIFEST GOD!

Leader: For in him the power of God's presence dwells!

People: AND FROM HIM THE LIGHT OF GOD'S GLORY POURS!

Collect

God of deepest mystery, time and again you have overcome the limitations of our minds and enlightened us as to your holy nature and will. Reveal yourself to us once more: that, inspired by your majestic holiness, we may become ennobled as your children and enabled as your servants. In Jesus' name we pray. Amen

Prayer of Confession

God of wondrous mercy, we regretfully confess that we often use the natural limitations of our human minds and our obvious inability to understand you fully as an excuse to ignore you completely. Forgive us, O God, and point us once again to your self-manifestation in the Christ. Transform us with the strength of his example, even as he was transfigured by the power of your presence. In his holy name we pray. Amen

Ash Wednesday

First Lesson: Joel 2:1-2, 12-17a

Theme: Felt repentance versus formal regrets

Exegetical note: The context for Joel's prophesies is a plague of locusts, which he interprets as a sign of God's approaching judgment ("the day of the Lord"), and takes as an opportunity to call the people to repent and return to their "gracious and merciful" God. The methods that he commends are public and traditional rituals: fasting, weeping, and mourning. But he insists that these acts reflect a deeply felt repentance (i.e., of "torn hearts") rather than a merely formal expression of regrets (e.g., with "torn garments").

Call to Worship

Leader: Brothers and sisters, we come before God this Ash Wednesday as sinful people.

People: BUT WE ALSO COME AS A REPENTANT PEOPLE, TRUSTING IN GOD'S MERCY!

Leader: For ours is a righteous and a merciful God!

People: OURS IS A JUST AND GRACIOUS GOD!

Collect

Just and righteous God, you have given us the opportunity to repent of our sins and to receive your mercy. Help us to use this special day to best advantage: that feeling in our hearts the deepest regret for our shortcomings, we may open ourselves completely to your forgiving grace in Jesus. In his name we pray. Amen

Prayer of Confession

Gracious and merciful God, we are deeply sorry that we are so sinful, and that we fail so miserably and consistently to live godly lives. We know that we deserve your wrath and your punishment. Please forgive us anyway, O God, out of the rich storehouses of your grace and mercy, and instill in us a spirit of true repentance and conversion, so that we may henceforth live holy lives devoted to you, your Christ, and your coming Reign. In the redemptive name of Jesus we pray. Amen

Ash Wednesday

Second Lesson: 2 Corinthians 5:20b—6:2 (3-10)

Theme: The immediacy of God's grace

Exegetical note: After expressing in a nutshell the essence of both his soteriology and his Christology (5:18-19, 21), Paul urges the Corinthian Christians not to take God's grace lightly, and insists that the salvation promised eschatologically by such prophets as Isaiah (quoted in v. 6:2a) is available in the present moment (the "now" of v. 6:2b).

Call to Worship

Leader: Behold, now is God's acceptable time!

People: NOW IS THE DAY OF SALVATION!

Leader: Let us therefore ready ourselves for God's reconciling grace!

People: LET US PREPARE OURSELVES TO RECEIVE GOD'S OWN RIGHTEOUSNESS IN CHRIST JESUS!

Collect

Most glorious God, you have declared today as your acceptable time, the very day of our salvation. Impress upon us the extent of our alienation from you: that, aware of the urgency of our need for reconciliation, we may be ready to receive your immediate redemption in Christ Jesus. In his name we pray. Amen

Prayer of Confession

Merciful God, it grieves us to recognize just how much we are alienated from you because of our sin, and how afflicted our lives are as a result. We would rather forget our sorry condition, and we postpone dealing with it as long as possible, as though our redemption were a last resort. Forgive us, we pray, and convince us of the urgency of our need and the immediacy of your reconciling, redeeming grace, which brings us the benefits of Christ Jesus, not in some obscure future, but in the here and now. In his name we pray. **Amen**

Ash Wednesday

Gospel: Matthew 6:1-6, 16-21

Theme: Christian penance as closet piety

Exegetical note: Jesus' (or Matthew's!) criticism here is directed, not at the three types of piety specified (almsgiving, prayer, and fasting), but at what must have been (and probably still is) the irresistible tendency to make these public spectacles for popular approval. The sayings recorded here, therefore, commend a kind of "closet penance," built on the conviction that acts of repentance should be private matters between the individual and God, and not exhibitions for public consumption.

Call to Worship
(based on Psalm 51)

Leader: May God have mercy upon us!

People: FOR WE KNOW OUR TRANSGRESSIONS, AND OUR SIN IS EVER BEFORE US!

Leader: Behold, God desires truth in the inward being!

People: MAY GOD THEREFORE PURGE US, WASH US, AND FILL US WITHIN!

Collect

Glorious God, you have taught us proper repentance through the words of Jesus. Teach us today the secret of self-examination: that, made deeply aware of the sinful condition of our inner spirits, we may feel the kind of contrition that will prepare us for the grace you offer in the Christ. In his name we pray. Amen

Prayer of Confession

Gracious God, we acknowledge and confess now with public words the sin and iniquity that we feel most profoundly in the privacy of our spirits, and that we feel powerless to overcome. We have made valiant attempts to change our ways, but often simply to appear religious or righteous to those around us. Forgive us, we pray, and enable us to repent in the privacy of our inner selves, with sincerity and singleness of heart. Then restore and reconcile us to you by the power of your Holy Spirit and your grace in the Christ in whose name we pray. Amen

First Sunday in Lent

First Lesson: Genesis 2:4b-9, 15-17, 25—3:7

Theme: Self-awareness as sin-awareness

Exegetical note: These excerpts from the Jahwist's version of creation and account of humanity's so-called "fall" should be read in light of recent revisionist interpretation, which treats the story, not as a literal-historical or Pauline-Augustinian account of the *cause* of sinfulness, which ruined a primodial state of human perfection, but as a mythical representation of the process by which every human comes to self-awareness of alienation from God.

Call to Worship
(based on Psalm 130)

Leader: Out of our depths we lift our voices to God!

People: MAY GOD HEAR AND LISTEN!

Leader: If God should number our inquities, who could bear it?

People: BUT GOD IS FORGIVING, AND HEEDS OUR CRIES FOR MERCY!

Collect

Great Creator God, you made us in your image and after your likeness to grow in godliness. Give us the strength of your Spirit: that, thus empowered, we may regain the innocence and righteousness that all of us have lost in our fall from grace and into sin. In the restorative name of Jesus we pray. Amen

Prayer of Confession

Most caring and good God, we confess with deep regret that we have fallen into sin and have failed to reflect your divine image as we should. We have experienced our own temptors, lost the innocence of our individual Edens, and lived lives of misery and malice as a result. Forgive us, we pray, and grant us the grace and renewed humanity offered us in the Christ, the second Adam, in whom alone we can become new creations of goodness and truth, justice and love. In his holy name we pray. Amen

First Sunday in Lent

Second Lesson: Romans 5:12-19

Theme: The "excessiveness" of God's grace

Exegetical note: This linguistically difficult passage has been interpreted through the eyes of Augustine so long that it is hard to extricate its original meaning from the layers of "Original Sin" theory that enshroud it. Taken on its own merits, however, Paul's statement seems to be affirming both the universality of sin and everyone's active participation in it and (therefore) responsibility for it. Likewise, as vv. 15-17 show, Paul's Adam-Christ parallel is unbalanced: the grace of God in Jesus is "excessive," for it does more than simply "undo" the curse of sin from Adam.

Call to Worship
(based on Psalm 130)

Leader: Let us wait upon God!

People: LET US HOPE IN GOD!

Leader: With God there is steadfast love!

People: WITH GOD THERE IS PLENTEOUS REDEMPTION!

Collect

God of exceeding goodness, you have given us in Christ Jesus more than enough grace to overcome the sin that plagues our lives. Assist us now by opening our hearts and minds, our souls and spirits to this precious gift: that, touched by its redemptive power, we may grow into the image of Jesus, in whose name we pray. Amen

Prayer of Confession

God of extraordinary grace, we acknowledge with sadness our responsibility for the condition of sin that dominates our lives, as well as for the many acts of sin that it produces; and we admit that, were you merely just and fair, and not gracious and merciful, we should suffer much more than we do as a result. Forgive us, we pray, and grant us from the rich storehouses of your mercy the grace that we need to become faithful and productive children of yours, purveyors of light and life rather than of darkness and death. In the saving name of Jesus we pray. Amen

March 11, 1990

First Sunday in Lent

Gospel: Matthew 4:1-11

Theme: Temptation as self-centered

Exegetical note: Although for Matthew the temptations of Jesus relate particularly to his messianic role, as a reading for the first Sunday in Lent, this passage speaks more clearly to the implications of the generic temptation that confronts every human where it touches us most closely: at the point of self-identity and self-definition.

Call to Worship

Leader: As a part of the human family, let us worship God!

People: AS BROTHERS AND SISTERS OF JESUS, LET US LIFT OUR SPIRITS IN PRAYER AND PRAISE!

Leader: As those who experience temptation, let us present ourselves to the Most High!

People: AS PEOPLE WHO KNOW THAT EVIL HAS BEEN OVERCOME, LET US APPROACH GOD IN HUMILTY AND GRATITUDE!

Collect

Heavenly God, you have created us above all creatures with a wonderful consciousness of ourselves and a marvelous potential for spirituality. Help us to seek and find our identities in you and your Word: that, properly centered, our lives may become holy, godly, and worthy to bear the name of the Christ, in which we pray. Amen

Prayer of Confession

Holy God, it pains us to confess just what messes our lives are as a result of our self-centeredness, and how futile and frivolous our many efforts at self-definition and self-help really are. We have tried to find ourselves in fads, philosophies, power, possessions, substances, superheroes, experts, and exercises, and still we feel off-center, aimless, and worthless. Forgive us, we pray, and help us through your Spirit to get into touch with the image of yourself that you have planted within us, and to remake it with the full humanity of Jesus as our model. In his name we pray. Amen

Second Sunday in Lent

First Lesson: Genesis 12:1-4a (4b-8)

Theme: God's outlandish promises

Exegetical note: This passage, which begins the Abraham narratives of Genesis, shows the great patriarch leaving his land in obedience and response to God's call and outlandish (but nonetheless eventually fulfilled!) promises, thereby setting into motion the history of the people of God — not only (as it turns out) the Israel that derived directly from him, but the New Israel, the Church, in which the promises were renewed and expanded.

Call to Worship
(based on Psalm 33)

Leader: The words of God are trustworthy!

People: THE WORKS OF GOD ARE FAITHFUL!

Leader: God loves righteousness and justice,

People: AND FILLS THE EARTH WITH STEADFAST LOVE!

Collect

Holy God of Israel, you called Abraham to become the father of a great nation. Grant us our own vocations and destinies in your plan, and the exceptional faith of that great man: that, hearing your extraordinary promises and incredible prospects for us, we may respond and find fulfillment as he did. In Jesus' name we pray. Amen

Prayer of Confession

Sustaining God of the Church, we confess to you our seeming inability to believe your Word or to respond faithfully to your commandments or your promises. We seek our own goals and destinies under our own powers, and find life empty and meaningless. Forgive us, O God, and grant us the grace and the faith of Abraham, so that we may follow your will and find our way to fulfillment and completion in you, your coming Reign, and your Christ. In his holy name we pray. Amen

Second Sunday in Lent

Second Lesson: Romans 4:1-5 (6-12), 13-17

Theme: Sharing the faith of Abraham

Exegetical note: Paul here substantiates his key notion of justification by faith (i.e., trust in God's grace) by appealing to Abraham as one who was justified, not by virtue of his works of obedience to the law, but because God graciously "reckoned" righteousness to him. That Paul regards Abraham as a model is obvious in v. 16, in which the patriarch is called "the father of us all," precisely because the promise that rests on grace is guaranteed to everyone who shares his faith.

Call to Worship
(based on Psalm 33)

Leader: Behold, the eye of God is upon all who hope in God's steadfast love!

People: AND GOD DELIVERS US FROM DEATH TO LIFE!

Leader: Our souls wait upon God!

People: AND WE TRUST IN GOD'S HOLY NAME!

Collect

God of wondrous love, you graciously called Abraham to an unconditional faith and an unbelievable future. Instill such a faith in us: that, drawn into an ongoing relationship with you, we also may realize the marvelous destiny that always awaits your people. In Jesus' name we pray. Amen

Prayer of Confession

God of boundless mercy, we confess that we do not really put our faith in you and your grace, but try instead to make our fortunes and build our futures through our own abilities and achievements; and we admit that we lead pointless and pitiful lives as a result. Forgive us, O God, and give us the faith of our father Abraham and our mother Sarah, who centered their lives and placed their hopes in your promises, and found fulfillment in your will and your word. In the name of the Christ we pray. Amen

Second Sunday in Lent

Gospel: John 3:1-17

Theme: The inspiring power of the cross

Exegetical note: The discourse that connects the basis for the most common expression of popular piety ("born again" in v. 3) and the most quoted verse of the New Testament (v. 16) is surprisingly cryptic. One of the clearest allusions is in v. 14, which recalls the serpent lifted up by Moses in Numbers 21:9ff., the very sight of which cured the Israelites of snake bite. The implication that merely beholding the crucified Christ cures sin points to the inspiring power of the cross.

Call to Worship

Leader: Sisters and brothers, let us speak of what we know!

People: LET US BEAR WITNESS TO WHAT WE HAVE SEEN!

Leader: God loved the world enough to give a Son!

People: THAT ALL OF GOD'S SONS AND DAUGHTERS SHOULD HAVE ETERNAL LIFE!

Collect

Almighty God, you loved the world enough to send a son, who loved the world enough to die. Set before us the image of the crucified Christ: that, moved by his compassion, we may find within us the kind of faith that brings health and life, not only to ourselves, but also to our sin-sick world. In his holy name we pray. Amen

Prayer of Confession

Good and gracious God, we confess that we often lose sight of the cross, the image of which should inform and inspire every moment of our lives; that we devote ourselves instead to images of worldly status and success; and that we thus seek salvation not in self-giving faith but in self-serving folly. Forgive us, we pray, and impress upon our imaginations the compelling image of the crucified Christ, which alone can bring the eternal life and perfect peace that you have promised all who believe. In Jesus' name we pray. Amen

Third Sunday in Lent

First Lesson: Exodus 17:3-7

Theme: Hardening hearts and testing God

Exegetical note: It is interesting that the only reference to this incident in the Old Testament (Psalm 95:8ff.) focuses on its negative aspect, namely, the fact that the people hardened their hearts and tested God. Paul, however, in 1 Corinthians 10:4 gives this event (and its parallel in Numbers 20:7ff.) a positive "spin" by equating the rock with none other than the Christ!

Call to Worship
(based on Psalm 95)

Leader: Come, let us sing to God!

People: LET US MAKE A JOYFUL NOISE TO THE ROCK OF OUR SALVATION!

Leader: Let us come into God's presence with thanksgiving!

People: LET US LAVISH GOD WITH SONGS OF PRAISE!

Collect

All-powerful God, you have put up with human unfaithfulness throughout history. Empower us with your Spirit: that, trusting at last in you and doing your will, we may live at peace with ourselves and one another. In the inspiring name of Christ Jesus we pray. Amen

Prayer of Confession

Most patient God, we confess with shame that, like the Israelites of old, we have tried you and tested you by breaking your commandments, ignoring your will, and doubting your word, and we have wound up wandering aimlessly in a spiritual wilderness of our own making. Forgive us, we pray; give us by your grace the desire and ability to commit ourselves fully and to entrust ourselves completely to you; and lead us finally into the promised glory of your coming Reign and the image of Christ Jesus. In his name we pray. Amen

Third Sunday in Lent

Second Lesson: Romans 5:1-11

Theme: Reconciliation to God

Exegetical note: After spelling out the effects of justification in the first few verses of this passage, Paul returns in vv. 6ff. to talk about justification itself in terms of the image of *reconciliation*, which presupposes that the state of sin is one of estrangement. Paul makes it clear in v. 10 that it is we who are reconciled to God by virtue of the Christ, rather than vice versa (as certain later theories of atonement suggested), presumably because alienation was humanity's problem, not God's.

Call to Worship
(based on Psalm 95)

Leader: O Come, let us worship and bow down!

People: LET US KNEEL BEFORE THE GOD OF OUR SALVATION!

Leader: For God is ours!

People: AND WE ARE GOD'S!

Collect

Eternal God, you have always found ways to reconcile estranged humanity to yourself. Return us to your good graces as well: that, restored to a meaningful relationship with you, we may become transformed after the image and likeness of the Christ. In his holy name we pray. Amen

Prayer of Confession

Merciful God, it shames us to have to admit how often we have turned our backs on you, how consistently we have ignored our relationship with you, how far we have drifted spiritually from you, and how much we have suffered as a result. Forgive us, O God, and remind us again of your reconciling grace in the person and work of Christ Jesus. Draw us once more to you, and keep us there forever by the sustaining power of your Holy Spirit. In the redemptive name of Jesus we pray. Amen

Third Sunday in Lent

Gospel: John 4:5-26

Theme: Quenching spiritual thirst

Exegetical note: The central point of this multifaceted incident between Jesus and the Samaritan woman hinges on the double entendre in the phrase "living water." Water imagery for spirituality is practically universal (e.g., as in Hinduism, Buddhism, and Taoism), but there was no doubt in the mind of John and the faith of the early Church that it was precisely (and only) Jesus, the Christ, who was the life-giving water.

Call to Worship
(based on Psalm 95)

Leader: In God's hands are the depths of the earth!

People: UNDER GOD'S CONTROL ARE THE HEIGHTS OF THE MOUNTAINS!

Leader: For God made the dry lands on which we may stand!

People: AND GOD MADE THE WATERS FROM WHICH WE MAY DRINK!

Collect

Magnificent God, your power and grandeur are like a mighty boundless ocean of infinite depth and purity. Let the waters of your Spirit wash over us and fill us: that, with our spirits cleansed and quenched, we may be refreshed and renewed. In Jesus' name we pray. Amen

Prayer of Confession

Compassionate God, we confess that, because of our sinful inclinations and acts, we lead parched lives with spirits that are dry as death and thirst for you. Forgive us, we pray; lead us as you did the Samaritan woman to the bottomless well of your living water, which you so freely offer us in Christ Jesus; and let us drink deeply there of your glorious grace, your matchless mercy, and your lasting love. In the name of Jesus, the Christ, the water of life, we pray. **Amen**

Fourth Sunday in Lent

First Lesson: 1 Samuel 16:1-13

Theme: God's "X-ray" vision

Exegetical note: The key contrast in this wonderful story of Samuel's anointing of David as God's hand-picked successor of Saul as king is contained in verse 7b, which declares that God's vision is very different from humanity's, in that the latter focuses on outward appearances, while God's "X-ray" eyes see the inner person: the heart, which is to say, the spirit. In the present case, God's first choice was Samuel's least likely candidate (and would have been ours as well).

Call to Worship
(based on Psalm 23)

Leader: God is our shepherd: we shall not want!

People: GOD GIVES US PLACES OF REST AND MEANS OF REFRESHMENT!

Leader: God leads us beside living waters and restores our souls!

People: GOD IS WITH US, AND WE ARE GOD'S PEOPLE! HALLELUJAH!

Collect

Most wise God, you have the power to see into our souls and to know our true spirits. Bring us to a better knowledge of ourselves: that, our illusions and delusions dispelled, we may know our shortcomings and open ourselves to your salvation in Christ Jesus, in whose name we pray. Amen

Prayer of Confession

Holy God, we confess with regret how consistently we avoid seeing ourselves and our fellow human beings for what we really are; how deliberately we rely on outward appearances; how successfully we fool ourselves and others into believing that we are leading happy, spiritual, and fulfilling lives; and how completely we thus ignore our need for your grace. Forgive us, we pray, and give us a measure of the power of your vision, which penetrates to the inner spirit and sees the real person, one yearning for your forgiveness and fulfillment. In the redeeming name of Jesus we pray. Amen

Fourth Sunday in Lent

Second Lesson: Ephesians 5:8-14

Theme: Waking from darkness, walking in light

Exegetical note: This passage was probably a part of catechetical instructions for baptisands in the primitive Church; hence, the sharp contrasts (e.g. "once . . . darkness, now . . . light"), which may echo some dualistic cosmologies that were current (e.g., Zoroastrianism's). But Paul's message is clearly Christocentric: like the rising morning Sun, the Christ shines on those sleeping in darkness (i.e., death!) and makes them children of light, who should "walk" (i.e., act) accordingly.

Call to Worship
(based on Psalm 23)

Leader: God is like a caring shepherd!

People: GOD LEADS US IN PATHS OF RIGHTEOUSNESS!

Leader: Christ Jesus is like the morning sun!

People: HE WAKES US FROM THE SLEEP OF DEATH AND BIDS US TO WALK IN THE LIGHT!

Collect

Great God of light, you have wakened our spirits from dark nights and made our souls to walk in broad daylight. Shine brightly upon us: that, basking in your glorious Spirit, we may truly live as children of light, and sisters and brothers of the Light. In his holy name we pray. Amen

Prayer of Confession

Most radiant God, we humbly confess that we often live as though our spirits were captives of the darkness of sin rather than beings upon whom you have shed a new, divine light; and that our deeds bespeak evil, not goodness. Forgive us, O God, and bring us once again out of the shadows. Set us aglow with the brightness of the one true Light, Christ Jesus, and make us and all of our acts reflect his brilliance. In his name we pray. Amen

Fourth Sunday in Lent

Gospel: John 9:1-41

Theme: Believing as seeing

Exegetical note: The miracle of the restoration of sight in this carefully-tailored narrative works at two levels: (1) at the literal, it is a mighty act that demonstrates the inbreaking of God's Reign and the identity of Jesus as the Messiah; and (2) at the figurative, it refers to the ability of this Christ to deliver people from spiritual blindness (as well as the capacity of some to choose blindness by rejecting him).

Call to Worship
(based on Psalm 23)

Leader: Let us enter God's house!

People: LET US SIT AT GOD'S TABLE!

Leader: Let us feast on God's abundant food!

People: LET US DRINK FROM GOD'S OVERFLOWING CUP!

Collect

God of wondrous miracles, you have relieved people of their infirmities throughout history. Heal now our spiritual blindness: that, the eyes of our souls made whole, we may at last set our sights on you, your Christ, and your coming Reign. In the name of Jesus we pray. Amen

Prayer of Confession

Holy and healing God, we confess with the deepest sorrow how intentionally and persistently blind we have been to your divine word and will for our lives, and how unrighteously and miserably we have lived as a result. Forgive us, we pray, restore to us our spiritual sight, and direct our vision thus renewed to the wonderful and inspiring image of your coming Kingdom, to the Christ who embodies it, and to the peace, hope, love, and justice that mark it as your new creation. In Jesus' holy name we pray. Amen

Fifth Sunday in Lent

First Lesson: Ezekiel 37:1-14

Theme: The life-breathing God

Exegetical note: This passage from the early exilic period records the well-known (through song) "dry bones" vision and its interpretation. The vision itself, with its reference to body and breath, seems to key on the creation story in Genesis 2. If the interpretation (vv. 11ff.) is any indication, the death here is a figurative reference to the sorry plight of Israel, so that the vision speaks not to resurrection in the specific sense, but to God's power to breathe life into even hopeless causes.

Call to Worship
(based on Psalm 116)

Leader: Let us love the God who hears our voices!

People: LET US CALL UPON GOD AS LONG AS WE LIVE!

Leader: Even when the throes of death and threats of hell surround us,

People: GOD HEARS AND BREATHES NEW LIFE!

Collect

Life-breathing God, you fashioned dead clay into the first humans and gave new life to Ezekiel's dry bones. Bring vitality to us and our world: that, being given the new possibilities that only you can offer, we may at least glimpse the divine Reign of yours that is to come through the Christ. In his name we pray. Amen

Prayer of Confession

God of hopeless causes, we confess that we often feel and act as though we were dead clay or dry bones that have never been touched by the life-giving benefits of your Christ or the revitalizing action of your Spirit. Forgive us, we pray, and fill us with life anew. Help us to overcome all of the death-dealing tendencies and traits in our individual, family, social and political lives, and make us agents of your living and life-bearing gospel. In the name of the Bread of Life we pray. Amen

March 25th

Fifth Sunday in Lent

Second Lesson: Romans 8:6-11

Theme: Realized resurrection

Exegetical note: Paul here speaks of the life-giving power of the Spirit in relation to the idea of resurrection. But instead of connecting the specific resurrection of Jesus to the future, eschatological, general resurrection of the dead, as he often does, he ties it to the new life that the Christian believer may realize here and now in this life as a release from the "death" that results from devoting oneself to things of the flesh (i.e., of this world).

Call to Worship
(based on Psalm 116)

Leader: Gracious and righteous and merciful is God!

People: GOD PRESERVES THE SIMPLE AND SAVES THE LOWLY!

Leader: God has delivered our souls from death, our eyes from tears, and our feet from stumbling!

People: GOD HAS MADE US WALK IN THE LAND OF THE LIVING!

Collect

God of boundless Spirit, you have declared in scripture and demonstrated in Jesus the power to bring life out of death. Revive us as well: that, the dead parts of our souls and lives thus resurrected, we may become living and breathing testimonies of your gracious ability to save. In Jesus' name we pray. Amen

Prayer of Confession

God of life-giving power, we acknowledge with the deepest regret the deadly hold that we allow the things of the world to have over us, and especially power, possessions, privilege, and prestige; and we admit the misery that we see and sow as a result. Forgive us, we pray, and help us to experience the spiritual resurrection that you offer us, not just after physical death, but during this life. Free us from all that entombs and enshrouds us, and makes us new creations after the example of Christ Jesus. In his holy name we pray. Amen

March 18, 1990

Fifth Sunday in Lent

Gospel: John 11:(1-16) 17-45

Theme: Jesus as life-giver

Exegetical note: John's account of Jesus' raising of Lazarus is in many ways a traditional miracle story. But the evangelist's placement of this event near the end of Jesus' earthly ministry and his addition of the dialogues and discourses give his own theological "spin" to the story. The key Christological assertion comes in Jesus' pronouncement in verses 25 and 26, which portray him as a life-giver, for both the dead and the living!

Call to Worship
(based on Psalm 116)

Leader: Let us offer to God the sacrifice of thanksgiving!

People: LET US CALL UPON GOD'S NAME!

Leader: Let us pledge ourselves to God in this congregation!

People: IN THE COURTS OF THE HOUSE OF GOD LET US LIFT OUR VOICES IN PRAISE!

Collect

Great Creator God, you sent Jesus the Christ as a life-giver for the dead and the living. Apply his revitalizing benefits to us: that, resurrected and renewed by his death-defying powers, we may ourselves become channels of your regenerative power and love for the rest of the world. In the name of Jesus we pray. Amen

Prayer of Confession

Death-defying God, we sadly confess that we are all like Lazarus, dead and rotting in tombs, though ours are made of sin and constructed by ourselves. Forgive us our preoccupation with death, O God, which turns us into walking corpses and our world into a graveyard at best, and at worst a hell. Help us to feel in our own lives the resurrection of spirit that only you can bring, and to channel to others the new life that is only yours to give. In the miraculous name of Jesus the Christ we pray. Amen

Sixth Sunday in Lent
(When observed as the Sunday of the Passion)

First Lesson: Isaiah 50:4-9a

Theme: The prophet's perilous profession

Exegetical note: This so-called Third Servant Song of Second Isaiah expresses the author's constant confidence in God despite the anger and abuse that he has had to endure, ostensibly at the hands of his fellow exiled Israelites, to whom his message of faith and hope sounds ridiculous. Yet, the Servant expresses both his determination to convey the message and his certainty of God's sustenance and eventual vindication.

Call to Worship
(based on Psalm 31)

Leader: Let us seek refuge in God!

People: MAY GOD'S RIGHTEOUSNESS DELIVER US!

Leader: May God hear us and rescue us!

People: MAY GOD BE OUR ROCK AND OUR RETREAT!

Collect

Steadfast God, you have always helped your servants to endure anger and abuse, harassment and hardship as they carried your word and will to the world. Sustain us as well: that, encouraged by your presence and power, we may be effective and unswerving witnesses of your grace and love. In Jesus' name we pray. Amen

Prayer of Confession

Sustaining God, it grieves us to confess how inconsistently we show confidence in you, your power to save the world, and your promise to vindicate those who serve you and your Word; and how easily we are discouraged, distracted, and deterred from doing your will by the least little aggravation or abuse. Forgive us our undependability and lack of heart, O God, and inspire us again with the examples of the prophets and the Christ, who, confident of your promises, served you steadfastly. In the name of Jesus we pray. Amen

April 1st.

Sixth Sunday in Lent
(When observed as the Sunday of the Passion)

Second Lesson: Philippians 2:5-11

Theme: The suffering Savior

Exegetical note: This passage contains an ancient Christian hymn appropriated by Paul as an example of how the Philippian Christians should comport themselves. The hymn reflects in many respects Gnostic savior mythology, but Paul seems to have added the phrase "even death on a cross" in v. 8 in order to underscore the very un-Gnostic notion that Jesus' humility and obedience culminated in a torturous execution and real death, on the basis of which God exalted him and his name.

Call to Worship
(based on Psalm 31)

Leader: Love God, all you saints!

People: GOD PRESERVES THE FAITHFUL!

Leader: Be strong! Take courage!

People: WE WAIT UPON GOD, OUR ROCK AND OUR REFUGE!

Collect

God of extraordinary power, you made your presence felt long ago in one emptied of divinity and subject to suffering and death. Teach us the miracle of self-sacrifice: that, emulating Jesus, we may become like him redemptive agents of yours, not despite our frail humanity, but because of it. In his humble but holy name we pray. Amen

Prayer of Confession

Most patient God, we confess that we do not always conduct ourselves as though we have within or among ourselves what Paul calls a "mind in Christ Jesus," but instead behave as though dancing to the world's tune or marching to society's drum. Forgive us, we pray, and inspire us again with the image of the one who emptied himself and was obedient to your word and will even, to the point of a torturous death, all so that a sin-sick world and a hell-bent humanity could come to know you and the presence and power of your coming Reign. In his holy name we pray. Amen

Sixth Sunday in Lent
(When observed as the Sunday of the Passion)

Gospel: Matthew 26:14—27:66

Theme: The Godforsakenness of the cross

Exegetical note: Matthew follows his source Mark very closely here, especially in preserving the drama of Jesus' anguished quotation of Psalm 22 in v. 27:46 as his last word and the climax of the Passion account. Although some interpreters would argue that that Psalm, taken in its entirety, bespeaks faith rather than a feeling of abandonment, the single phrase "cried" from the cross clearly suggests otherwise, and underscores the paradoxical power of the whole event.

Call to Worship
(based on Psalm 31)

Leader: Blessed is God, who has shown us wondrous and steadfast love!

People: EVEN WHEN WE ARE ASSAILED AND ASSAULTED!

Leader: Even when we feel abandoned and alone!

People: GOD HEARS OUR PRAYERS AND DELIVERS US!

Collect

Everlasting God, you are always with us in steadfast love, even when we feel most abandoned and afraid. Strengthen our faith in you by the power of your Holy Spirit: that, fortified from within, we may do every sacred task and make any terrible sacrifice that service to you requires. In Jesus' name we pray. Amen

Prayer of Confession

Everloving God, we confess with dismay that we often take the moments of Godforsakenness that we all feel from time to time as an excuse to abandon our ministry and mission in service to you, and to do instead works and deeds of self-service and self-enrichment. Forgive us our inconstancy, we pray, and set our sights so firmly on the image of your coming Reign that we shall never falter or fail in fulfilling our duties as those who bear the name of the crucified Christ. In his spirit and name we pray. Amen

Sixth Sunday in Lent
(When observed as Palm Sunday)

First Lesson: Isaiah 50:4-9a

Theme: From palms to Passion

Exegetical note: The unpopularity of the prophet in this Third Servant Song of Second Isaiah, not to mention the anger and abuse that he has experienced, appears to differ markedly from Jesus' triumphal entry into Jerusalem. If the palm-wavers were sincere (rather than sarcastic, as some suggest), their adoration was short-lived: their cries of exaltation soon became calls for execution.

Call to Worship
(based on Psalm 118)

Leader: This is the day that God has made!

People: LET US REJOICE AND BE GLAD IN IT!

Leader: This is God's house and the gateway to righteousness!

People: BLESSED ARE THOSE WHO ENTER IN GOD'S NAME!

Collect

Almighty God, you sent us a Christ whom we exalted and then executed. Give us at last the spirit of steadfastness: that, deeply devoted to you, your Word, and your will, we may remain faithful despite the twists and turns of events and the peaks and valleys of our emotions. In the trustworthy name of Jesus we pray. Amen

Prayer of Confession

Most merciful God, we confess how fickle our faith is, and how much we are like those ancient palm wavers, who quickly turned from praising, hailing, and extolling you, your Christ, and your Reign, and became cynical betrayers and traitors. For we have likewise broken trust and sold out to this or that promising idea, fad, or leader. Forgive us, we pray, and so fill us with your Spirit that we shall never stray from the Way that leads to life eternal for ourselves and our world. In the precious name of Jesus we pray. Amen

Sixth Sunday in Lent
(When observed as Palm Sunday)

Second Lesson: Philippians 2:5-11

Theme: The paradoxical procession

Exegetical note: The ancient Christian hymn contained in this passage speaks of both the humility and the exaltation of the savior, and in that respect speaks eloquently to the paradox inherent in the event of Jesus' triumphal entry, which combined the regal and the ridiculous, majesty and mockery, stateliness and simplicity. Such a procession into the Holy City seems calculated to claim power and authority at the same time that it caricatures it.

Call to Worship
(based on Psalm 118)

Leader: Blessed is the one who enters in God's name!

People: BLESSINGS FROM THE HOUSE OF GOD!

Leader: God has given us light!

People: LET US APPROACH GOD'S ALTAR WITH THANKS FOR GOD'S GOODNESS!

Collect

God of all authority, you sent a Christ who with humility and simplicity put the world's powers and principalities in their place. Give us a respect for true majesty: that, unimpressed by earthly claims, we may stand in proper awe of you and your coming holy Reign. In the regal name of Jesus we pray. Amen

Prayer of Confession

Eternal God, we confess our tendency to be fascinated with and to admire the rich and famous, the powerful and prestigious, the influential and impressive, and to ignore the values of humility and simplicity taught and lived by Jesus even through his triumphal entry into Jerusalem on a donkey. Forgive us our vacillation, O God, and help us to recapture a proper sense of priorities, which hold dear your coming Reign and the virtues of peace, hope, love, and justice that it promises. In the sacred simplicity of the name of Jesus we pray. Amen

Sixth Sunday in Lent
(When observed as Palm Sunday)

Gospel: Matthew 21:1-11

Theme: Seeing God's Reign in the Christ

Exegetical note: Matthew makes a noteworthy departure from his source Mark in this account of Jesus' triumphal entry when in v. 9 he changes his predecessor's "Blessed is the coming Reign of our father David" (Mark 11:10) to "Hosanna to the Son of David!" That shift in focus from the Reign to the Christ reflects the transition in emphasis in the early Church from the teachings of Jesus to the message about Jesus, precisely because the earliest believers saw in his deeds the active Reign of God.

Call to Worship
(based on Psalm 31)

Leader: Blessed is the coming Reign of our father David!

People: AND BLESSED IS THE ONE WHO COMES IN GOD'S NAME!

Leader: Hosanna to the Son of David!

People: HOSANNA IN THE HIGHEST!

Collect

God of might, you made known the presence of your coming Reign in a humble person, Jesus. Help us to know in him your presence and power: that, seeing you and your sovereignty embodied in one like us, we may adjust our values and priorities in accordance with your will. In Jesus' name we pray. Amen

Prayer of Confession

Almighty God, we admit with regret our fondness for pomp, pretense, and pageantry, and our tendency to mistake these for real importance and power; and we therefore confess that we would have been among those shouting and waving palms at Jesus' triumphal parade, and calling for his crucifixion a few days later when the trappings were gone. Forgive us, we pray, lead us beyond superficial appearances to the substance and spirituality of the Christ event, and impress us with the reality of your presence in this humble **carpenter's son**, in whose name we pray. Amen

Monday in Holy Week

First Lesson: Isaiah 42:1-9

Theme: Christ's ministry of light and liberation

Exegetical note: This passage contains the so-called "First Servant Song" of Second Isaiah (vv. 1-4) and an elaboration upon it (vv. 5-9). The song itself focuses on the qualities of the Servant, while the elaboration is more concerned with the scope of his mission, which can be summarized in the words "light" and "liberation."

Call to Worship

Leader: Blessed is God's Servant, who brings light to the nations!

People: BLESSED IS GOD'S CHOSEN ONE, WHO BRINGS LIBERATION TO THE CAPTIVE!

Leader: In his name, let us worship the God of Israel!

People: IN HIS NAME, LET US WORSHIP THE GOD OF ALL CREATION!

Collect

Most radiant God, you sent your Servant to bring light to the nations. Make him a lamp for our way as well: that, our paths illuminated by his brilliance, we may advance along the road to righteousness established by his life and death. In his redeemiing name we trust and pray. Amen

Prayer of Confession

Liberating God, it saddens us to confess to you the extent to which we allow ourselves to fall captive to sin and Satan, as well as to the powers and principalities of this world, and to admit our resulting failure to experience or embrace the perfect freedom into which you have always led your people. Forgive us, we pray, and help us to use this Holy Week as an opportunity to appropriate the benefits offered us in Christ Jesus, especially the release from spiritual bondage that his death made possible. In his name we pray. Amen

Monday in Holy Week

Second Lesson: Hebrews 9:11-15

Theme: The ultimate atonement

Exegetical note: This passage amounts to a radicalization of the images of priest and sacrifice that dominate the Christology of the entire epistle. In this case, the Christ makes the ultimate atonement by entering the Holy of Holies (i.e., God's presence) and sacrificing himself (an unblemished offering), thereby effecting "an eternal redemption" and everlasting purification that negates even death itself.

Call to Worship

Leader: In the name of Jesus, the Christ, let us lift our hearts to God!

People: IN THE NAME OF JESUS, OUR HIGH PRIEST, LET US PRAISE GOD'S HOLY NAME!

Leader: In the name of Jesus, the unblemished lamb, let us give thanks for our salvation!

People: IN THE NAME OF JESUS, WHOSE SELF-SACRIFICE IS OUR ATONEMENT, LET US TRUST AND HOPE!

Collect

Eternal God, you sent us in Christ Jesus a high priest who could make a perfect sacrifice for our atonement. Help us in this Holy Week to accept his action on our behalf: that, cleansed thereby of our sin, we may live lives of holiness and justice worthy of his redeeming love. In his holy name we pray. Amen

Prayer of Confession

Compassionate God, it is painful to admit how consistently we resist and refuse the effects of Jesus' incredible atoning self-sacrifice, and how completely we instead remain dominated and directed by sin. Forgive us, we pray, empower us by your Holy Spirit to accept at last the cleansing and redeeming benefits of his priestly offering, and assist us in leading lives that befit those for whom the bonds of sin have been broken and the debts of sin have been paid. In the name of the Christ we trust and pray. Amen

Monday in Holy Week

Gospel: John 12:1-11

Theme: Impending tragedy, ultimate triumph

Exegetical note: The Fourth Evangelist's version of the anointing of Jesus at Bethany differs from those of his predecessors by identifying the woman as Mary as well as by mentioning Lazarus, whose emergence from the grave John has just recounted (11:38-44). Mary's act of anointing (as told here, at least) is, of course, a symbolic preparation of Jesus for burial, while the reference to Lazarus prefigures both Jesus' death and his ultimate resurrection.

Call to Worship

Leader: Let us begin this Holy Week with a sense of tragedy.

People: FOR JESUS, THE CHRIST, MUST SOON SUFFER AND DIE!

Leader: But let us maintain this week a sense of triumph!

People: FOR IN JESUS' DEATH IS REDEMPTION, AND IN THAT REDEMPTION IS OUR HOPE!

Collect

Most Holy One, you taught us in the life of Jesus to look beyond life to death, and beyond death to life eternal. Grant us the vision to see the world and our existence from your eternal perspective: that, thus enlightened, we may see beyond all our tragedies your ultimate triumph. In the name of Jesus we pray. Amen

Prayer of Confession

Most merciful God, we confess our tendency to dwell on the negative aspects and tragic events of our lives and of those around us, and even to wallow in the feelings of despair and hopelessness that they trigger in us, with the result that we feel bad about human nature in general and ourselves in particular. Forgive us, O God, and teach us to trust, even in the most heart-rending tragedies and gut-wrenching injustices, that you are at work, graciously drawing life and redemption out of death and damnation. In the name of Jesus and in the shadow of his cross we pray. Amen

Tuesday in Holy Week

First Lesson: Isaiah 49:1-7

Theme: The Christ's all-encompassing mission

Exegetical note: The first six verses of this selection comprise what is called the Second Servant Song of Deutero-Isaiah, which identifies the servant with the people of Israel, whose universal mission has been (figuratively speaking) from the womb. New Testament writers (e.g., Luke 2:32, Acts 13:47 and 26:23, Galatians 1:15) saw here a reference to the Christ's all-encompassing mission, for which he was destined even prior to his birth.

Call to Worship

Leader: We gather today as servants of the Christ!

People: WE MEET AS FOLLOWERS OF JESUS, WHOSE MISSION BEGAN IN MARY'S WOMB!

Leader: We worship as disciples of that Nazarene, whose ministry was for all humankind!

People: IN HIS GLORIOUS NAME, LET US GIVE PRAISE AND THANKS TO GOD!

Collect

Eternal God, you called from the womb the prophets and then the Christ to bring your gracious word of redemption to all humankind. Bless us now with their universal vision and compassion: that, seeing beyond our narrow boundaries, we may learn to show love and concern even for those least like us. In the spirit of Jesus we pray. Amen

Prayer of Confession

Most compassionate God, we confess that even during this Holy Week we find it all too easy to apply the benefits of the life and death of Jesus to ourselves and those most like us, and to fail to see in him your love for all humankind. Forgive us our selfishness and narrowness of vision, we pray, and broaden and deepen our compassion, so that it better resembles the boundless scope of your mercy and the bottomless depths of your love. In the name and the cross of the Christ we pray. Amen

Tuesday in Holy Week

Second Lesson: 1 Corinthians 1:18-31

Theme: The "foolishness" of faith

Exegetical note: The Greek philosophical tradition had apparently left its impression on the Corinthians, for Paul here finds it necessary to shake their confidence in their own wisdom and knowledge. His claim here is that redemption and righteousness reside in God's "foolishness," i.e., the weak, lowly, despised, and crucified Christ.

Call to Worship

Leader: Let us worship the God of righteousness!

People: LET US WORSHIP THE GOD WHO REDEEMS!

Leader: For ours is a God whose weakness overcomes all of the world's powers!

People: OURS IS A GOD WHOSE FOOLISHNESS CONFOUNDS ALL OF THE WORLD'S WISDOM!

Collect

Life-giving God, you have taught us to embrace a "foolish" faith in a Christ who was lowly, gentle, despised, and finally killed by the powers and authorities of his day. Teach us at last to embrace such faith: that, in the face of all the world's "sane" values and "sensible" claims, we may still trust in your incredible love. In the spirit of Jesus we pray. Amen

Prayer of Confession

God of love, we admit that we often feel and show contempt for the very characteristics displayed by the Jesus whom we claim to serve: humility, gentleness, selflessness, poverty, and pacifism; and we even find ways to baptize their opposites and call them "Christian." Forgive us, we pray, and teach us to look always to the image of the despised, defeated, and finally dead "loser" on the cross, and to see there our only true model of human success, triumph, victory, and achievement: a life given in selflessness to you and humankind. In the name of the Christ we pray. Amen

Tuesday in Holy Week

Gospel: John 12:20-36

Theme: The glory of Golgotha

Exegetical note: This passage has the feeling of a kind of "hodgepodge" drawn together (but not very tightly!) by John. The clearest image here is his distinctive view of the crucifixion of Jesus as a glorification rather than a humiliation, an experience of exaltation rather than of passion. The initial request of the Greeks (Gentiles) to see Jesus is merely a literary "set-up" for that powerful image.

Call to Worship

Leader: Sisters and brothers, if you would see Jesus, behold the cross!

People: FOR THE CHRIST WHO REDEEMS IS THE ONE CRUCIFIED THERE!

Leader: Disciples of the Christ, if you would follow him, you must be drawn to his glory!

People: AND HIS GLORY IS THAT OF GOLGOTHA!

Collect

Everliving God, you gave us a glimpse of glory on Golgotha in a suffering Savior. Help us now to set our eyes and hearts on him: that, reliving his crucifixion, we may see not only his humiliation and execution, but his glorification and exaltation in service to your will and coming Reign. In his redeeming name we pray. Amen

Prayer of Confession

Eternal God, we confess our seeming inability to grasp your many mysteries, and particularly the subtleties of your self-manifestation in a suffering Christ, executed as a criminal. We admire worldly "winners" and success stories, and despise the very kinds of "bleeding hearts" and "do-gooders" that most emulate Jesus. Forgive us, we pray, and help us finally to adjust our values in such a way that we shall at last be able to look beyond appearances of weakness and defeat to behold your strength and victory. In the name of Jesus we pray. Amen

Wednesday in Holy Week

First Lesson: Isaiah 50:4-9a

Theme: Suffering as integral to Servanthood

Exegetical note: In this so-called "Third Servant Song" of Second Isaiah, the servant (apparently an individual here rather than the collective Israel as elsewhere) has suffered on account of his divine calling, and anticipates doing so in the future; still he exhibits certainty of receiving God's eventual help and vindication.

Call to Worship

Leader: Let us worship in the name of God's special servant!

People: LET US WORSHIP IN THE NAME OF ONE WHO SUFFERED!

Leader: Let us worship in the knowledge that service to God means suffering to follow!

People: LET US WORSHIP IN CONFIDENCE THAT SUCH SUFFERING BRINGS ULTIMATE BLESSING!

Collect

Almighty God, your servants have always suffered by doing your will, but in the certainty of ultimate vindication. Give us just such confidence: that, secure in our faith in you, we may willingly confront all the dangers and endure all the hardships that service to you seems to bring. In the name of the crucified Christ we pray. Amen

Prayer of Confession

Compassionate and loving God, we confess that we look to the cross as simply the destiny of Jesus, and refuse to see, much less accept, suffering as part and parcel of discipleship to him and service to you, your word, and your will. Forgive us, we pray, and place in our hearts both the recognition that those who truly serve you must suffer at the hands of a misunderstanding world, and the willingness and courage to endure whatever we must in loving you and following Jesus. In his holy name we pray. Amen

Wednesday in Holy Week

Second Lesson: Hebrews 12:1-3

Theme: The crucifixion as inspiration

Exegetical note: The writer here conceives Old Testament luminaries as a crowd of spectators at a "race of faith," whose prize is joy. The runners are facilitated by the encouragement of these witnesses, as well as inspired by Christ's having completed the course on the cross. The suffering Jesus is thus appealed to as the model contestant against sin, weariness, and faintheartedness.

Call to Worship

Leader: Fellow contestants in the race of faith, let us look to those who have gone before!

People: LET US CONSIDER THE GREAT SAINTS OF ISRAEL!

Leader: Let us behold the godly Servant of Nazareth!

People: INSPIRED BY THEIR EXAMPLES, LET US COMPLETE THE COURSE THAT IS BEFORE US!

Collect

Magnificent God, you have raised great saints to serve you faithfully in every generation, and a Christ who was faithful unto death. Set our eyes on this great crowd of witnesses: that, encouraged by their example, we may run the course of faith more swiftly and finish the race of life victorious in you. In Jesus' name we pray. Amen

Prayer of Confession

Most merciful God, we confess our tendency to lose heart and grow weak in the race of faith, to let the world and the concerns of everyday life overtake and defeat us, and to allow the message of the cross that salvation comes by struggle and suffering to fade from our minds. Forgive us our lack of perseverance and endurance, O God, and bestow upon us the strength of your Holy Spirit, which alone can bear us to an eternal victory and everlasting prize. In the name of the crucified Christ we pray. Amen

Wednesday in Holy Week

Gospel: John 13:21-30

Theme: Betraying the beloved Christ

Exegetical note: John alone among the evangelists has Satan entering Judas only after the latter has received the bread from Jesus, raising the interesting possibility that the bread was not just an indication of Judas' prior intention out of malice, but indeed a symbol of Jesus' commissioning of a trusted one as the betrayer! Still, John clearly wants to contrast that role with that of the other "beloved" disciple, for whom betrayal would have been unthinkable.

Call to Worship

Leader: Rejoice, Christians, for our Christ is easy to love!

People: JESUS ATTRACTED FOLLOWERS BY THE POWER OF HIS PERSON!

Leader: But remember, disciples, that one who loved him also left him!

People: MAY WE NEVER BETRAY OUR BELOVED CHRIST!

Collect

Great God, you have set before us in scripture the images of both believers and betrayers. Help us to choose the former as our models: that, when times of crisis and demands for decision arise, we may stand firmly with the faithful. In Jesus' name we pray. Amen

Prayer of Confession

Gracious God, we confess with the deepest sorrow and regret that, as often as not, we have betrayed — in thought, word, and deed — the very Christ to whom we have pledged our allegiance, and have caused suffering to his body, the Church. Forgive us, we pray, and help us to take this Holy Week as a precious opportunity to renew our faith, to deepen our commitment, and to resolve ourselves never to do anything that will deviate from Jesus' teachings, detract from his ministry, or defame his sacrifice on our behalf. In his name we pray. Amen

Maundy Thursday

First Lesson: Exodus 12:1-14

Theme: God's Lamb, God's liberation

Exegetical note: When the Synopticists (especially) depicted Jesus as celebrating the Seder meal with his disciples as his last intimacy with them, they (and perhaps he) were certainly drawing upon the symbolic connection between Moses' leading the Israelites out of Egyptian captivity, depicted in this lesson, and the Master's own liberation of humanity from enslavement to sin.

Call to Worship
(based on Psalm 89)

Leader: Let us sing of God's steadfast love!

People: LET US PROCLAIM GOD'S FAITHFULNESS TO ALL GENERATIONS!

Leader: For God's steadfast love was established forever!

People: AND GOD'S FAITHFULNESS IS AS FIRM AS THE HEAVENS!

Collect

God of perfect freedom, you led the Isrealites out of captivity through Moses and us out of captivity through Jesus. Help us to internalize the liberty that you have given: that, no longer bound by sin, we may live lives of righteousness that show that Jesus did not die in vain. In his name we pray. Amen

Prayer of Confession

God of liberating love, it pains us deeply to admit the extent to which we still live as though in bondage to sin instead of reveling in the freedom that you have graciously granted us in the cross of the Christ. Forgive us, we pray, and teach us at last to embrace the benefits of Jesus, his life and his death, and to live henceforth as people who have been set free by your mercy and love and made righteous by your Servant's selfless act of obedience and compassion. In his precious name we pray. Amen

Maundy Thursday

Second Lesson: 1 Corinthians 11:23-26

Theme: A memorial meal and more

Exegetical note: Although Paul's version of the Last Supper here is earlier than those of the Gospels, it is more stylized than the Synoptic accounts in the way it parallels the bread and cup. Both statements contained here emphasize the memorial aspect of the meal, but verse 26 entails a future, eschatological reference as well: it is a meal of proclamation "until."

Call to Worship
(based on Psalm 89)

Leader: Let the heavens praise God's wonders!

People: LET THE CONGREGATION PRAISE GOD'S FAITHFULNESS!

Leader: For who is as mighty as God?

People: AND WHO IS SO SURROUNDED WITH STEADFAST LOVE?

Collect

Nourishing God, you have provided us through Jesus' example a common meal rich in significance. Make its bread and wine refreshment for our souls and encouragement for our hearts: that, feeling here the presence of Christ Jesus, we may trust and hope until he brings your heavenly Reign in all its fullness. In his name we pray. Amen

Prayer of Confession

Nurturing God, we confess our habitual failure to take seriously the rituals in which we participate, including the Supper instituted by Jesus in this Holy Week. We eat of the bread half-heartedly and drink of the cup absent-mindedly, and seldom manage to feel his presence or your grace there. Forgive us, we pray, and renew our appreciation for this most precious gift. Enrich our weak spirits with your Holy Spirit, so that we may experience in this and every eucharist a communion, not only with one another, but also with you. In Jesus' name we pray. Amen

Maundy Thursday

Gospel: John 13:1-15

Theme: The cleansing crucifixion

Exegetical note: John's account of the Last Supper differs from the Synoptics in placing it on the day before the actual Passover meal and in recounting a footwashing, an act that for the evangelist symbolically entwines two principal symbolic themes: cleansing and mutual submission. The former of these appears to refer mainly to the import of Jesus' crucifixion for the disciples, while the latter bespeaks the attitude that the disciples should display to one another.

Call to Worship
(based on Psalm 89)

Leader: Blessed are those who walk in God's light!

People: BLESSED ARE THOSE WHO REJOICE IN GOD'S NAME!

Leader: For they exalt in God's name all day long!

People: AND IN GOD'S RIGHTEOUSNESS THEY ARE EXALTED!

Collect

God of eternity, you have taught us in the footwashing of Holy Thursday that the way of the Christ is not status, but submission. Instill this lesson in our hearts: that, following the example of Jesus, we may seek to serve you by serving one another in humility and gratitude. In Jesus' name we pray. Amen

Prayer of Confession

God of tender mercies, we acknowledge with shame that our customary and cherished way of life is based on a selfish desire for status and not a consistent yearning to serve one another and others in accordance with your will and Jesus' example. Forgive us, we pray, and teach us true humility and sacrificial service. Place before us always the image of the Christ, who, despite the supernatural majesty of his divinity, submitted himself in service, not only to his closest disciples, but indeed to all humanity. In his name we pray. Amen

Good Friday

First Lesson: Isaiah 52:13—53:12

Theme: The suffering substitute

Exegetical note: This Fourth Servant Song is not without its difficulties, not the least of which is the identity of the servant (the prophet? the Messiah? Israel?). In any case, the Servant is innocent, and yet bears all these afflictions and those of all others as well, to their redemption. Whether or not this passage predicted Jesus' Passion, or shaped his attitude toward it, since the early Church, Christians have seen in it the essence of that event.

Call to Worship
(based on Psalm 22)

Leader: May God be not far from us!

People: MAY GOD HASTEN TO HELP US!

Leader: May God deliver us!

People: MAY GOD SAVE US!

Collect

Holy God, you sent one who was innocent to suffer in our stead for our sin. Make us deeply aware and appreciative of his sacrifice: that, taking to heart that wonderous gift, we may become the kind of people that his death enables us to be. In his precious name we pray. Amen

Prayer of Confession

Gracious God, we confess that we deny, ignore, and disguise our sin and guilt, and expend a great deal of energy feigning innocence and goodness, when in fact we know how truly sin-riddled our lives are. Forgive us, we pray, and open us to the tremendous gift of love and mercy that the suffering of Christ Jesus brought. Convince us once and for all that he suffered so that we don't have to, and that we are righteous in your eyes only because he was indeed. In his holy name we pray. Amen

Good Friday

Second Lesson: Hebrews 4:14-16, 5:7-9

Theme: Offering obedience

Exegetical note: This passage builds on a central theme of the high priesthood of Christ Jesus. In that capacity, he did what humanity was expected to do, but because of sin could not do, namely, offer to God (in addition to prayers, supplications, cries, and tears) perfect obedience. In so doing, he redeemed all who then would offer him obedience, which is, if not perfect, at least now acceptable.

Call to Worship
(based on Psalm 22)

Leader: Let all the ends of the earth remember and turn to God!

People: LET ALL THE FAMILIES OF THE NATIONS WORSHIP BEFORE HIM!

Leader: For dominion belongs to God!

People: GOD RULES OVER THE NATIONS!

Collect

Most glorious God, you gave us in Christ Jesus one who could make the acceptable offering for sin that we could not. Make us deeply grateful for his work and your mercy: that, touched by the enormity of his act, we may be moved to live lives that reflect its redemptive effects in obedience to your will. In Jesus' name we pray. Amen

Prayer of Confession

Most gracious God, it troubles us to admit, to you or ourselves, just how self-righteous we are, trusting in our basic human goodness rather than your divine grace, and how we continue to wallow in sin as a result. Forgive us, we pray, and turn our attention back to the holy work of Christ Jesus, our perfect high priest, and his offering to you. Convince us at last that, if we are worthy and acceptable in your eyes, it is only because he was. In his name we trust and pray. Amen

Good Friday

Gospel: John 18:1—19:42 or John 19:17-30

Theme: The Christ's ultimate victory

Exegetical note: With these two chapters John's peculiar slant on the crucifixion as a glorification reaches its climax, and produces a singularly passionless Passion! Jesus is in quasi-regal control throughout the narrative and discourses, and many details attest or suggest his royal stature. At the end, he gives orders from the cross, and even commands his own expiration. This is not the tormented, anguished, writhing Jesus depicted by the mystical or liberation traditions, but a triumphant *Christus victor.*

Call to Worship
(based on Psalm 22)

Leader: God is holy, enthroned on the praises of Israel!

People: IN GOD DID OUR MOTHERS AND FATHERS TRUST!

Leader: They trusted in God and were not disappointed!

People: THEY TRUSTED IN GOD AND WERE SAVED!

Collect

God of all mystery, you sent one of a strange kind of royalty to bring us from sin to salvation. Help us now to contemplate his cross: that, seeing there a victory rather than a defeat, we may be moved again by his tragedy and inspired by his triumph. In his redemptive name we pray. Amen.

Prayer of Confession

God of all mercy, we confess how hard it is, despite all of our pious claims, for us to feel deeply the death of one person so many centuries ago, or to take seriously the impact that it is supposed to have on our lives. Forgive our scepticism, O God, and touch our thoughts and feelings with the great drama of Jesus' crucifixion. Make us to see and to remember always that whatever righteousness we have, it is because of this one's victory on the cross over the powers of sin and death. In the name of Jesus and the confidence of othe cross we pray. Amen

The Resurrection of Our Lord
(Easter Day)

First Lesson: Acts 10:34-43

Theme: Easter as God's "Yes"

Exegetical note: The heart of the kerygmatic recapitulation contained in Peter's speech to Gentiles here is his view of the resurrection (in v. 40) as God's validation of Jesus after the crucifixion. The latter was the "no" of humanity (designated with an indefinite "They") to Jesus' ministry, while Jesus was God's resounding, and ultimately prevailing "Yes."

Call to Worship
(based on Psalm 118)

Leader: God is our strength and song!

People: GOD HAS BECOME OUR SALVATION!

Leader: We therefore shall not die!

People: WE SHALL LIVE TO RECOUNT GOD'S MIGHTY ACTS!

Collect

Gracious God, you have given us in Jesus' resurrection your most profound affirmation over all that would destroy us. Make us receptive and responsive to your Word of grace: that, our every obstacle overcome, we may lead new lives of purpose and peace. In the name of the Christ we pray. Amen

Prayer of Confession

Most merciful God, we confess that our ears and hearts are often closed to your divine affirmation of us, and that we therefore live in subjection to self-depreciation and guilt, feeling wretched and worthless. Forgive us, we pray, and set our eyes once again this Easter Day upon the empty tomb of Christ Jesus. Help us to see there your profound "Yes" to our lives and our very natures, over against all of the world's powers and principalities that would negate and destroy us. In the name of the resurrected Christ we pray. Amen

The Resurrection of Our Lord
(Easter Day)

Second Lesson: Colossians 3:1-4

Theme: The incompleteness of the Resurrection

Exegetical note: Paul still has in mind baptism as a symbolic participation of the believer in Jesus' death and resurrection. The point he wants to make in these verses is that the raising of Jesus is not the end of the story. For one thing, there is the ethical demand placed on those "raised with Christ." For another, there is the appearance of that same Christ at the *parousia*, which suggests that the Christian's life until then remains "hidden with Christ in God."

Call to Worship
(based on Psalm 118)

Leader: Thanks be to God, who has become our salvation!

People: THANKS BE TO GOD, WHO HAS GIVEN US A GREAT LIGHT!

Leader: God has opened to us the gates of righteousness!

People: LET US ENTER THROUGH THEM AND GIVE THANKS!

Collect

Living God, you have given us new life in the death and resurrection of Jesus. Help us to see that great gift as a beginning rather than an end: that, responding to your grace, we may grow in faith and works until your risen one returns. In his name we pray. Amen

Prayer of Confession

Life-giving God, we confess our tendency to be complacent, and even smug, in our status as children of the resurrection, and to forget your expectation that we who have been given the possibility of new life must actually live new lives in response. Forgive us, O God, and inspire us anew with the image of the resurrected Jesus. Let it stir us and move us to wholeness and holiness, to the end that we ourselves shall become evidence of the truth of the resurrection of the Christ. In his holy name we pray. Amen

The Resurrection of Our Lord
(Easter Day)

Gospel: Matthew 28:1-10

Theme: Women as witnesses of the risen Christ

Exegetical note: Among the many nuances added to Mark's earlier resurrection account by Matthew's redaction is a heightening of the role of the women in the event. Mark had ended his account (in its original version) at 16:8, with the women's fearful silence. Matthew, however, has the women departing with joy, not fear, and bearing the first testimony to the fact of the resurrection, having been commissioned as witnesses not only by an angel, but by the risen Jesus as well!

Call to Worship
(based on Psalm 118)

Leader: This is the day that God has made!

People: LET US REJOICE AND BE GLAD IN IT!

Leader: Blessed are those who enter in God's name!

People: LET US GIVE THANKS FOR GOD'S GOODNESS AND STEADFAST LOVE!

Collect

God of all miracles, you revealed the resurrection of Christ Jesus first to women of faith. Help us to emulate their witness, that, beholding your mighty victory of life over death, we may be moved as they were to testify to your majesty, mercy, power, and grace. In the name of the resurrected Christ we pray. Amen

Prayer of Confession

God of all mercies, we are sorry to admit how feeble our witness to the resurrection of Christ Jesus really is. We affirm it in our hearts, but bear little testimony to it either in our words or our lives, which often have the appearance and odor of death rather than of new life. Forgive us, we pray, and set before us again the fact of the open tomb and empty grave. Fill us with resurrection power and renewed life, so that we may at last reflect the glow of that first Easter dawn. In the name of the risen Christ we pray. Amen

Second Sunday of Easter

First Lesson: Acts 2:14a, 22-32

Theme: God's paths of life

Exegetical note: This selection recounts a portion of Peter's first kerygmatic "sermon" in Acts. The death and resurrection of Jesus are, of course, the double focus, the main point being that the latter has overcome the former. In the process, Luke has Peter quoting Psalm 16 to make clear that the resurrection means that God's love and power have proven to be stronger than the worst kind of human alienation, death and Hades, and have offered instead "paths of life" and divine "presence."

Call to Worship
(based on Psalm 16)

Leader: Let our hearts rejoice! Let our souls be glad!

People: LET OUR BODIES DWELL SECURE!

Leader: For God has not abandoned us to death!

People: GOD HAS SHOWN US THE PATH OF LIFE!

Collect

Eternal God, you gave us in the resurrection of Jesus a path to life. Set our feet upon that holy way: that, walking at last at your direction, we may journey toward the holiness and righteousness that befit all those who travel in the company of the Christ. In his name we pray. Amen

Prayer of Confession

Everliving God, we confess with the deepest regret that we do not always walk in your paths to life as companions of the risen Christ, but instead try to make our own way; and we acknowledge how much we wander aimlessly through life and how lost we often become as a result. Forgive us, we pray; plant our feet firmly upon your holy way and guide our every step with your eternal Light. Make our destination eternal life and our directions to that end clear and compelling. In the name of Jesus we pray. Amen

Second Sunday of Easter

Second Lesson: 1 Peter 1:3-9

Theme: New life, unfinished faith

Exegetical note: This passage was probably drawn from a baptismal setting in which the symbolization of death and resurrection was central. In any case, the focus here is on the new birth made possible by Jesus' having been raised, but the main point is that in this new life the faith is unfinished, being tempered while awaiting eschatological completion in salvation at "the last time," i.e., the *parousia*. Meanwhile, the reborn may have some suffering to endure.

Call to Worship
(based on Psalm 16)

Leader: May God, our Refuge, preserve us!

People: FOR APART FROM GOD WE HAVE NO GOOD!

Leader: Those who choose other gods multiply their sorrows!

People: BUT WE HAVE CAST OUR LOT WITH GOD! HALLELUJAH!

Collect

God of ageless wonder, you have made us heirs to eternal life in the resurrection of Jesus. Help us to see our faith as unfinished: that, embracing the spiritual vitality that you have given us, we may yet continue to grow into the image of the risen Christ, in whose name we pray. Amen

Prayer of Confession

God of amazing grace, we acknowledge and confess that we like to make faith a static thing, an accomplished fact, rather than a living and growing relationship with you, made possible by Jesus' resurrection. Forgive us, we pray, and convince us anew that our faith is unfinished as long as we live in a world of time and space and until Jesus comes in glory. Help us to begin to realize the new potential and possibilities that you opened to us when that Easter stone rolled away. In the name of the risen Christ we pray. Amen

Second Sunday of Easter

Gospel: John 20:19-31

Theme: Hearing is believing

Exegetical note: John's inclusion of the "doubting Thomas" episode appears to be addressed to the Church of his own day, which did not have direct evidence of the resurrection. The "punchline" on the lips of Jesus in verse 20, therefore, is directed, not so much at Thomas as to those second and third generation Christians who had access to the resurrected Christ only through the proclaimed kerygma. For them, *hearing* (or, according to v. 31, reading!) had to be believing.

Call to Worship

Leader: Sisters and brothers, we gather to hear the gospel of Jesus Christ!

People: WE MEET TO LEND OUR EARS TO HIS GOOD NEWS!

Leader: Blessed be the first disciples, for whom seeing was believing!

People: AND BLESSED ARE WE, TO KNOW OF THE RISEN CHRIST THROUGH THEIR TESTIMONY!

Collect

Most holy God, you have given us the testimony of scripture so that we who cannot see the risen Christ may believe through hearing. Open our hearts and minds to its message: that, moved by its power, we may also become witnesses to the truth that Jesus lives. In his name we pray. Amen

Prayer of Confession

Merciful God, we confess with regret our reluctance to believe in your miracles, even the ones we can see in the present; and we admit how much more difficult it is to believe what we have heard and have read about your mysterious and wondrous workings in the past, including the resurrection of Jesus. Forgive us, we pray, and give us a measure of the faith of the first disciples. Teach us to trust our hearts as well as our eyes, and our spirits as well as our hands; and above all strength our faith in the fact of the resurrection of Jesus. In his name we pray. Amen

Third Sunday of Easter

First Lesson: Acts 2:14a, 36-41

Theme: The Holy Spirit as a resurrection gift

Exegetical note: This selection contains the final part of Peter's Pentecost "sermon" on the resurrected Christ, and a rather urgent inquiry on the part of his would-be Christian hearers concerning the appropriate response. His reply is that they should repent and be baptized, and he promises them the gift of the Holy Spirit. It is noteworthy that, despite the tremendous numbers who reportedly accepted Peter's invitation, no mention is made of the earlier experience of "tongues" as accompanying the gift.

Call to Worship
(based on Psalm 116)

Leader: Let us lift up the cup of salvation!

People: LET US CALL UPON GOD'S NAME!

Leader: Let us pledge ourselves to God,

People: IN THE PRESENCE OF ALL GOD'S PEOPLE!

Collect

Great God, you have bestowed upon us in Jesus' resurrection both life and the promise of your Spirit. Make us worthy of these great gifts: that, having received such divine grace, we may learn to reap their benefits and grow to embrace their rewards. In Jesus' name we pray. Amen

Prayer of Confession

Gracious and loving God, we admit with shame that our natures are such that we want all of the rewards of the resurrection and none of the responsibilities; and that we would gladly take the eternal life, but ignore the expectations that it brings. Forgive us, we pray, and restore our spirits to such wholeness that, in addition to the life you have given, we shall also accept the Spirit that you have bestowed, which alone can sanctify us toward the wholeness of the risen Christ. In his precious name we pray. Amen

April 29th

Third Sunday of Easter

Second Lesson: 1 Peter 1:17-23

Theme: Faith and fear

Exegetical Note: The author is here exhorting his Christian readers to godliness, and in so doing suggests a precarious, paradoxical position for them: on the one hand they are indeed "ransomed" by Jesus' blood and made confident in God, but on the other hand they are still in "exile" and thus must remain fearful, which in this case probably does not mean merely bearing holy respect and awe for God, but rather maintaining a heathly anxiety about the evil, sin, and temptation that surround them until the *parousia* (which is always in the background in this epistle).

Call to Worship

Leader: Rejoice, Christians! For you have been ransomed by Jesus' blood!

People: PRAISE GOD FOR THE CHRIST, MADE MANIFEST FOR OUR SAKE!

Leader: Through him you have confidence in God!

People: THROUGH HIM WE HAVE FAITH AND HOPE!

Collect

God of majesty, you have ransomed us from sin in Christ Jesus. Let us not now be conformed to this world: that, aware of the darkness and evil that still surround us, we may remain mindful of their power and resistant to their influence until your Reign comes in its glory. In Jesus' name we pray. Amen

Prayer of Confession

God of mercy, we confess that we often live with a false sense of confidence as a result of our faith; that we take lightly the powers of darkness and death; and that we repeatedly fall into sin as a result. Forgive us, we pray, and plant in us a holy anxiety that will keep us on guard against all in the present unredeemed world that threatens resurrection life, until the next appearance of the Christ and the full realization of your coming Reign. In the name of Jesus we pray. Amen

Third Sunday of Easter

Gospel: Luke 24:13-35

Theme: The unrecognized Christ

Exegetical note: The Emmaus story may not have been a resurrection appearance in its original form, but only rendered so by Luke, for whom it becomes one more bit of testimony to the truth of the miracle. The most intriguing aspect of the story is that resurrected Jesus goes unrecognized until he breaks bread with them, whereupon, in retrospect, they realize that their hearts actually knew him when he expounded scripture to them. Nevertheless, by the time they come to full awareness of his identity, he has vanished.

Call to Worship

Leader: Let us worship the God of the earthly Jesus!

People: LET US WORSHIP THE GOD OF THE RISEN CHRIST!

Leader: But let us also prepare ourselves to encounter that same Christ,

People: EVEN WHEN HE IS DISGUISED AS THE LEAST OF OUR SISTERS AND BROTHERS!

Collect

Most Holy One, you manifested your power over sin and death in the raising of Jesus. Help us to recognize the living Christ in our lives: that, perceiving him even when he hides himself in the least of our kind, we may respond always in faith and love. In his holy name we pray. Amen

Prayer of Confession

Heavenly God, we confess that we live one-dimensional lives that are insensitive to your presence and that of the living Christ in the world; that we wind up directing our attention to all the wrong places and placing our faith in all the wrong things; and that we act in unholy and unwholesome ways as a result. Forgive us, we pray, and make us attentive and able to see with our hearts through the superficial to the spiritual, and to find in the creation around us the living Christ to touch us. In his name we pray. Amen

Fourth Sunday of Easter

First Lesson: Acts 2:42-47

Theme: The Church as community

Exegetical note: The picture of the earliest Church painted here refers almost exclusively to its life "in house" rather than its mission (e.g., the edifying *didache* is mentioned rather than the *kerygma* addressed to the non-believers). The fellowship (*koinonia*) in verse 42 is elaborated with the subsequent reference to fellowship, prayers, community of property (a primitive communism!), and communal meals — all portraying a charismatic community, not yet an institution, in which sharing is spontaneous and thoroughgoing.

Call to Worship
(based on Psalm 23)

Leader: Our God is a gracious host!

People: GOD CALLS US TO DINE AT A HEAVENLY FEAST!

Leader: God anoints us with the soothing and fragrant oils!

People: MAY GOD'S GOODNESS AND MERCY FOLLOW US, AND MAY WE DWELL IN GOD'S HOUSE FOREVER!

Collect

God of harmony, you have given your Church the possibility of a life together in Christ. Teach us to be a true community: that, having learned at last to love and to share, we may become a godly family and a fellowship of prayer. In the name of our brother Christ Jesus we pray. Amen

Prayer of Confession

God of healing love, we confess with shame how little we as your people reflect the kind of spiritual community portrayed in scripture as the ideal for the Church, and how broken we leave the body of the Christ as a result of our selfishness and pettiness. Forgive us, we pray, and fill us with your Spirit of love and harmony. Teach us to look beyond our narrow self-interests and toward the image of your coming Reign, in which fellowship and sharing will be complete because the love of Jesus will have made us one. In his name we pray. Amen

May 6th

Fourth Sunday of Easter

Second Lesson: 1 Peter 2:19-25

Theme: Suffering slaves and straying sheep

Exegetical note: This selection presents two images, both rather foreign to the experience of most modern readers: a slave who is beaten unjustly (either by the master or in the master's stead), and straying sheep. Yet, somehow these images are timeless, the former speaking to the human experience of the absurdity of life (and especially its unjust and untimely tragedies), and the latter addressing the typical experience of alienation or estrangement.

Call to Worship
(based on Psalm 23)

Leader: Our God is a protective shepherd!

People: UNDER GOD'S CARE, WE ARE SAFE AND SECURE!

Leader: Even when we walk through valleys of death, surrounded by enemies,

People: OUR GOD LEADS THE WAY TO QUIET AND REST!

Collect

God of all infinity, you experienced through Jesus our human feelings of alienation and absurdity in the face of life's troubles and tragedies. Give us the assurance of your presence and compassion: that, comforted by the knowledge that you understand, we may find strength and courage for the journey ahead. In Jesus' name we pray. Amen

Prayer of Confession

God of all intimacy, we admit that, despite our claim to Christian faith and hope, we allow ourselves to be overwhelmed and to fall into despair whenever the seeming injustices and inconsistencies of life confront us; and that we allow such things to draw us away from you rather than closer to you. Forgive us, we pray, and inspire us with true trust and complete confidence in you. Help us to see behind all of the darkness that assails us the glow of your love that affirms us. In the name of Christ Jesus we pray. Amen

Fourth Sunday of Easter

Gospel: John 10:1-10

Theme: The believer's intimacy with Jesus

Exegetical note: The mixture of "shepherd" and "door" images for Jesus in this passage suggests two originally separate sayings of Jesus fused and interpreted by the evangelist. The more accessible, though dated, image is that of the shepherd (vv. 1-6 and again in 8 and 10ff.), the point of which here is the intimate relationship of trust between the care-giver and the cared-for: they know and heed his voice, while he protects their lives with his very life.

Call to Worship
(based on Psalm 23)

Leader: God is our shepherd, leading us in paths of righteousness!

People: GOD GIVES US GREEN PASTURES FOR REST AND STILL WATERS FOR REFRESHMENT!

Leader: Jesus is also like a shepherd, whose voice we recognize and trust!

People: AND LIKE A GOOD SHEPHERD HE WILLINGLY GAVE HIS LIFE FOR THOSE IN HIS CARE!

Collect

Almighty God, you gave us a Good Shepherd who protected our lives by sacrificing his. Make us deeply appreciative of his compassion: that, moved by his selfless love, we may learn to care for one another after his example. In his name we pray. Amen

Prayer of Confession

Most merciful God, we confess that our self-centeredness and selfishness keep us from trusting one another or you as much as we should, as well as from being willing or even able to live sacrificially toward one another or those in need. Forgive us, we pray, and conform us to the image of the Good Shepherd, our Christ Jesus, who knew our faults and failings, loved us anyway, and willingly gave all for our safety, security, and salvation. In his precious name we pray. Amen

Fifth Sunday of Easter

First Lesson: Acts 7:55-60

Theme: The active, ascended Christ

Exegetical note: Stephen's vision of the ascended Christ in heaven prior to his own martyrdom is curious for two reasons: 1) his use of the phrase "Son of Man," otherwise used in the New Testament almost exclusively only by Jesus (but cf. Rev. 1:13, also in a vision!) and with eschatological if not apocalyptic overtones; and (2) his image of the Christ standing rather than sitting at God s right hand. What both of these suggest is a Christ not resting on his laurels but ready to become active, either to receive the spirit of the martyr-to-be or, more likely, to inaugurate the judgment of the end time.

Call to Worship
(based on Psalm 31)

Leader: Let us seek refuge in God!

People: MAY GOD NEVER LET US BE PUT TO SHAME!

Leader: May God give ear to us!

People: MAY GOD RESCUE AND PROTECT US!

Collect

Everlasting God, You sent us a son of humanity to act on our behalf for our salvation. Let his redemptive power continue to work for us: that, touched constantly by his love, we may ourselves become worthy daughters and sons of you. In the name of the Christ we pray. Amen

Prayer of Confession

Everliving God, we confess that we use the image of the exalted Christ seated at your right hand as an excuse to rest on his laurels and to be righteously inactive; and we admit that we often pray and wait for his second coming only as a way of shirking our Christian responsibility to be active in his name. Forgive us our passivity and laziness, O God, and fill us with your Spirit and a sense of the Christ's dynamic presence, which alone can inspire us to do the work of your coming Reign against all odds in this troubled world. In Jesus' name we pray. Amen

Fifth Sunday of Easter

Second Lesson: 1 Peter 2:2-10

Theme: God's transforming power and mercy

Exegetical note: Whoever this letter's real author was, it certainly does reflect what often appears to be the great Apostle's tendency to put his foot in his mouth. Here he jumbles and mixes three metaphors: newborn babies, living (?!) stones, and the New Israel (although he doesn't quite call it that). The most important theological thing he says comes in verse 10, after even he appears to have given up on his dubious images: God's power and mercy are utterly transforming.

Call to Worship
(based on Psalm 31)

Leader: God is our rock of refuge!

People: GOD IS THE FORTRESS OF OUR SAFETY!

Leader: Let us commit our spirits into God's hands!

People: LET US WORSHIP THE FAITHFUL GOD WHO HAS REDEEMED US!

Collect

God of creative might, you have transformed us and all humanity with your power in the Christ. Continue to recreate us through your Holy Spirit: that, changed gradually into the image of Jesus, we may know and do your divine will, even as he did. In his name we pray. Amen

Prayer of Confession

God of manifest mercy, we confess our ongoing resistance to your power to transform us from our present condition as slaves to sinfulness and captives to confusion, and our unwillingness to lay aside our pointless endeavors and meaningless lives in order to become righteous and holy people, empowered and eager to do your will. Forgive us, we pray, and open us up to your gracious desire and offer to change us into new creatures. Make us long for the image of the Christ until we are finally ready to accept your tender mercies and abundant new life. In the name of Jesus we pray. Amen

handwritten: May 13th

Fifth Sunday of Easter

Gospel: John 14:1-14

Theme: Apocalypse now

Exegetical note: This passage begins three chapters of Jesus' "farewell discourses," which follow directly the foot-washing and "new commandment." Among several distinctively Johannine themes here is the notion of Jesus' "coming again" presented in verse 3. But its elaboration does not occur until vv. 15ff., where it becomes clear that what John has in mind is not an event of the distant future, but rather precisely the gift of the Holy Spirit, which, in effect, makes the apocalypse a "now" event for both the evangelist and us.

Call to Worship
(based on Psalm 31)

Leader: Let us rejoice and be glad for God's steadfast love!

People: GOD SEES OUR AFFLICTIONS AND KNOWS OUR ADVERSITIES!

Leader: God does not deliver us into the hands of our enemies!

People: GOD DOES GIVE US FIRM-FOOTING, HOWEVER TROUBLESOME OUR PATHS!

Collect

God of every moment, you have guaranteed your Church the ongoing presence of the Christ through the power of your Spirit. Sensitize us to the movements of this Comforter: that, invigorated by its energy, we may become and remain the Body of the Christ at work in the world. Amen

Prayer of Confession

God of the eternal now, we confess that we often find a misplaced comfort in the remoteness of the Christ, and use his apparent absence from this earth and the seeming unlikelihood of his imminent return as excuses to accept the world as it is and only dream of how it might be. Forgive us our passivity, O God, and set us on fire with your Holy Spirit, so that our own souls will burn with a desire to experience your Reign over the earth in our day and our age. In the name of Jesus we pray. Amen

Sixth Sunday of Easter

First Lesson: Acts 17:22-31

Theme: Seeking the God who is near

Exegetical note: One interesting aspect of Paul's well-known Areopagus speech is his suggestion in verses 26ff. that God made humanity for the purpose of a religious quest, namely, that they might seek after and find God. The irony that Paul suggests, however, is that God is actually very near. Indeed, his first quotation in verse 28, whether from the pre-Socratic Epimenides or not, actually (and no doubt unintentionally) appears to compromise the transcendence of God that is the basis of biblical theism, and to suggest images more akin to Oriental religions than to Judaeo-Christianity.

Call to Worship
(based on Psalm 66)

Leader: Let all the earth make a joyful noise unto God!

People: LET ALL THE WORLD SING THE GLORY OF GOD'S NAME!

Leader: For great is God's power!

People: AND WONDROUS ARE GOD'S DEEDS!

Collect

Most exalted God, you have not remained aloof but drawn close to us in the person of Jesus. Make your presence felt as well in the power of your Holy Spirit: that, feeling you near, we may be both comforted and coaxed to do your will. In the name of Jesus we pray. Amen

Prayer of Confession

Merciful God, we confess that we often do not feel close to you, not because you have removed yourself from us, but because we have alienated ourselves from you, as well as from one another. Forgive us, we pray, and help us by your grace to overcome every kind of estrangement that our sinful nature causes. Teach us the meaning of atonement as at-one-ment, and bring us to just such a relationship of unity with you and community with one another by virtue of the merits of the Christ. In his name we pray. Amen

Sixth Sunday of Easter

Second Lesson: 1 Peter 3:13-22

Theme: The Church as God's ark

Exegetical note: After encouraging his readers — probably newly baptized Christians or candidates for baptism — to be ready to suffer in good conscience for their faith with the crucified Christ as their model, Peter (or pseudo-Peter) suggests in verses 20ff. that, as Noah and his family were saved by (rather than from!) the water of the legendary flood, so Christians are saved by the water of baptism. However dubious the logic of his portrayal of that anticie scenario, the idea of the Church as an ark of salvation that floats on the waters of baptism is still compelling.

Call to Worship
(based on Psalm 66)

Leader: Let us all bless God!

People: LET THE SOUND OF GOD'S PRAISE BE HEARD!

Leader: For God has kept us among the living!

People: GOD HAS NOT LET US SLIP OR FALL!

Collect

Great God, you have given us in the Church an ark in which we can ride out the floods of sin and evil that threaten our very lives. Help us to cherish this holy vessel: that, safe within the security it affords, we may help to guide it to the shores of your holy Realm. In Jesus' name we pray. Amen

Prayer of Confession

Most Holy God, we confess that we have seen the Church that you have provided us less as a ship of mercy than as a luxury liner on a pleasure trip, on which we have a good time without any concern about our Christian course or our divine duty. Forgive us our lack of direction and purpose, O God, and guide us across the perilous seas of life to the promised land of safety and security, urging us to pause only to rescue the many along the way who have been shipwrecked by sin. In the name of our great navigator, Christ Jesus, we pray. Amen

Sixth Sunday of Easter

Gospel: John 14:15-21

Theme: The ever-present Christ

Exegetical note: John's Gospel has a characteristic "realized eschatology," in which, with Jesus' giving of the Spirit, the *parousia* has, in effect, been accomplished. Accordingly, the present passage suggests that under the "counsel" of the invisible, indwelling Spirit, believers will be able to see Jesus when others do not and, further, that the ever-presence of the Christ will be life giving. Indeed, verse 20 suggests a relationship between God and believers (and Jesus) so intimate as to threaten the dualistic God-human distinction of Judaeo-Christian theism.

Call to Worship

Leader: Sisters and brothers, let us worship the ever-present God!

People: LET US PRAISE THE GOD WHO NEVER DESERTS US!

Leader: Let us bless the God whose Spirit is within us!

People: LET US GLORIFY THE GOD WHOSE EVER-LIVING CHRIST IS AMONG US!

Collect

Most loving God, you have made the Christ ever-present to give us abundant life. Open our eyes and hearts to his continuing presence: that, attuned to his ongoing care, we may ourselves become graciously present to others in his name, in which we pray. Amen

Prayer of Confession

God of parental love, we confess how closed and insensitive we let ourselves become in the face of all that the world has to stimulate us, and how conscious we are of the constant presence of the Christ, which would grace our lives if only we let it. Forgive us, we pray, and break down every barrier that insulates us from his powerful love and gentle strength, to the end that, under his influence, we may be conformed to his likeness and thus restored to your image. In his name we humbly pray. Amen

Ascension Day
(or the Sunday nearest)

First Lesson: Acts 1:1-11

Theme: The Church's mission in time and space

Exegetical note: With this beginning to what is, in effect, his Volume Two, Luke epitomizes his Gospel and lays the foundation for his recounting of the Apostles' Acts. The point of the inquiry and ensuing dialogue and angelic exhortation is to point to the future mission of the Church and, beyond that, to the return of Jesus. But the phrase "to the end of the earth" (v. 8) suggests that Luke now sees the delay of the *parousia* as a fact of life, giving the church plenty of time — and space — for mission.

Call to Worship
(based on Psalm 47)

Leader: Let all the people of the earth clap their hands!

People: LET ALL THE WORLD SHOUT AND SING!

Leader: For the most high God is wondrous to behold!

People: OUR MOST HOLY GOD RULES THE EARTH!

Collect

Exalted God, you received the ascended Jesus in heavenly places when his work on earth was done. Help us now to receive the Spirit he promised and sent: that, while we yet await the final coming of the Christ, we may use the time and space that you have given us to carry your Word to the world. In Jesus' name we pray. Amen

Prayer of Confession

Dearest God, we confess with shame how much we waste the opportunies that you have given us between the comings of the Christ, and how lightly we have taken what should have been an urgent mission on behalf of you, your Word, and your coming Reign. Forgive us, we pray, and empower and enthuse us with your Spirit to carry the gospel to every corner and nation of the earth. In his name we pray. Amen

Ascension Day
(or the Sunday nearest)

Second Lesson: Ephesians 1:15-23

Theme: The immeasurable greatness of God's power

Exegetical note: Sandwiched (or perhaps "buried") in the hopelessly rambling prayer contained here (in a single sentence with a barrage of genitives!) is the assertion of "the immeasurable greatness" of God's power in believers, as evidenced in the resurrection and ascension of Christ Jesus, with whom and through whom God has shared that "greatness of power," to the benefit of the Church, Christ's body.

Call to Worship
(based on Psalm 47)

Leader: Let us sing praises to God!

People: LET US SING PRAISES TO THE ONE WHO REIGNS OVER ALL CREATION!

Leader: For God rules the earth!

People: AND ALL NATIONS BOW BEFORE THE ONE EXALTED GOD!

Collect
Most mighty God, you raised Jesus and lifted him to your right hand. Keep us ever mindful of your consummate power over the world; that, as your Church and the Christ's body, we may become a redemptive force in mission to the world and formidable opponents of all the forces of death and destruction that threaten its people. In the exalted Christ's name we pray. Amen

Prayer of Confession

Glorious God, we admit how often we forget your awesome power over the world, which you shared first with Christ Jesus, and then with us through the Holy Spirit; and we acknowledge how weak and powerless we feel in the face of the sin in ourselves and the evil in the world as a result. Forgive us, O God, and impress us again with your limitless strength as well as the boundless capabilities that we would have, if only we opened ourselves to you. In the name of Jesus we pray. Amen

Ascension Day
(or the Sunday nearest)

Gospel: Luke 24:46-53

Theme: Waiting on the supporting Spirit

Exegetical note: Luke's version of Jesus' ascension is not as detailed as his one in Acts 1, but gives pretty much the same picture. Jesus sets before the disciples a formidable task: to preach repentance and forgiveness to the world. But, instead of sending them out immediately, he instructs them to return to Jerusalem to await the divine power (identified in Acts as none other than the Spirit) that will support their efforts.

Call to Worship

Leader: Let us prepare ourselves to celebrate a great moment in the Church's life!

People: FOR IT IS ASCENSION DAY, WHEN JESUS LEFT HIS DISCIPLES COMMISSIONED AS APOSTLES TO THE WORLD!

Leader: His instructions to them are also ours to follow: to build the Reign of God!

People: LET US AWAIT THE POWER OF THE HOLY SPIRIT AS WE PRAISE AND WORSHIP GOD!

Collect

Almighty God, you instructed the first apostles through the ascending Christ to prepare for their mission by awaiting the Spirit. Help us to heed that advice as well: that, properly reinforced from above, we may do your will and work with the efficiency and effectiveness that only your divine energy can insure. In Jesus' name we pray. Amen

Prayer of Confession

God of relentless grace, we confess our tendency to do your work, if at all, precipitously and under our own steam, rather than after being spiritually empowered by you; and we admit that our efforts are usually weak and our results often poor. Forgive us, we pray, and teach us to long for and wait upon your Holy Spirit, which alone can make us effective in ministry for you, your Christ, and your coming Reign. In the name of Jesus we pray. Amen

Seventh Sunday of Easter

First Lesson: Acts 1:6-14

Theme: The inclusiveness of discipleship

Exegetical note: This passage depicts the ascension of Jesus and the time immediately afterward, before the coming of the Holy Spirit (Acts 2), which would signal the real birth of the Church. Noteworthy here, on the basis of vv. 12-14, is the fact that they are already a community, staying together and praying together; and that community, moreover, is inclusive. Not only are the male disciples named, but the women are specifically mentioned, which, for an age that greatly undervalued women, signals an extraordinary role and status for them as equal partners in the nascent Church.

Call to Worship
(based on Psalm 68)

Leader: Let the righteous be joyful!

People: LET US EXULT BEFORE GOD!

Leader: Let the righteous be jubilant!

People: LET OUR HEARTS JUMP FOR JOY!

Collect

Almighty God, you called men and women to be equal partners in discipleship to the risen Christ. Teach us now to follow your bidding and his example: that, free of the stereotypes that we have inherited, we may accept all people as sharers with you in the building of your coming Reign. In Jesus' name we pray. Amen

Prayer of Confession

Good God of all, we confess that we often let prejudices of all kinds stand in the way of ministry and mission in your name: we ignore people's gifts and callings because of their sex, race, class, and age; and in so doing, we hamper the work of spreading the gospel of the Christ. Forgive us our biases, O God, and help us to overcome them with the power of your Spirit and the example of Jesus, who called even those deemed unacceptable by others to be members of his holy body. In his precious name we pray. Amen

Seventh Sunday of Easter

Second Lesson: 1 Peter 4:12-14, 5:6-11

Theme: Rejoicing in suffering

Exegetical note: With this passage, the author seems to narrow his focus from generalities about suffering for the sake of righteousness to specific sufferings that his readers have endured or may endure. In this context, he tells them to rejoice in their sufferings (v. 13) in the knowledge that they are shared by the Christ and in anticipation of eventual triumph and glory, the prospect of which is further spelled out in vv. 5:6ff.

Call to Worship
(based on Psalm 68)

Leader: Sing to God! Sing praises to God's name!

People: LIFT UP A SONG TO THE ONE WHO RIDES UPON THE CLOUDS!

Leader: That one is God!

People: REJOICE IN GOD'S NAME!

Collect

Most high God, you have taught us in scripture to rejoice in sufferings with faith and hope. Give us the wisdom and courage to do so: that, confident in your final victory over sin and death, we may endure whatever pain and hardship our discipleship demands. In the name of Jesus we pray. Amen

Prayer of Confession

Comforting God, we confess that we avoid pain and hardship at all costs, but especially when discipleship to Christ Jesus would seem to demand it; and that we instead serve your gospel only when our lives and livelihoods, our comforts and convenience, and our properties and priorities are not at stake. Forgive us, we pray, and teach us to rejoice in whatever sufferings our ministry brings, in the confidence that, whatever we have to bear or forfeit in this life for the Christ's sake will pale before the victories and joys of your coming Reign. In the name of the Christ we pray. Amen

Seventh Sunday of Easter

Gospel: John 17:1-11

Theme: The life-giving career of the Christ

Exegetical note: This so-called "high priestly prayer" serves as Jesus' retrospective dedication of his career, his request to be restored to his former (i.e., primordial) glory, and his blessing upon the disciples who will be left "in the world" after his death and again after his ascension. Verses 2 and 3 make explicit what has been the implicit purpose in Jesus' ministry all along, namely, to give eternal life, which here is equated with knowledge of God and the Christ.

Call to Worship
(based on Psalm 68)

Leader: Blessed is God, who daily supports us!

People: BLESSED IS GOD, WHO FINALLY SAVES US!

Leader: For ours is a God of salvation!

People: OURS IS A GOD WHO FREES US FROM DEATH!

Collect

Most generous God, you sent us a Christ whose career was life-giving. Grant us the wisdom and grace to accept his great gift: that, with everything that deals death in our lives overcome, we may live in ways that bestow life on others as well. In the name of Jesus we pray. Amen

Prayer of Confession

O God our help in every age, it pains and shames us to confess how much of what we do works toward the demise of our planet and the death of its inhabitants. We fill its air with pollutants and its waters with waste; we deplete the earth's resources, and even turn some of these into weapons of hideous destruction. Forgive us our death-dealing ways, O God, and sensitize us to the death-defying nature of your will and your Word. Help us to follow the example of Jesus in sowing life instead of death, and in bringing life out of death. In his name we pray. Amen

The Day of Pentecost

First Lesson: Isaiah 44:1-8

Theme: God's life-giving Spirit

Exegetical note: Deutero-Isaiah here uses poetic nature-imagery to express hope for the exiled and captive people of Judah to be restored from Babylonian captivity to their own Palestine. The image of God's Spirit as a life-giving water (rain?) poured out onto an arid soil (a dire situation) to revitalize a "parched" (hopeless) people is especially appropriate for Pentecost.

Call to Worship
(based on Psalm 104)

Leader: Without God's Spirit, we are as dust!

People: WITHOUT GOD'S SPIRIT WE ARE DRY AND PARCHED!

Leader: With God's Spirit, we are recreated!

People: WITH GOD'S SPIRIT WE ARE REFRESHED AND RENEWED!

Collect

Nurturing God, you have time and again poured out your life-giving Spirit upon people whose souls were dry and barren. Send us once more that Great Comforter: that, on this Pentecost Day, we may be revitalized by the renewing rain of your holy presence and power. In the name of Jesus we pray. Amen

Prayer of Confession

Compassionate God, we know that our lives are spiritually parched and that our souls thirst for meaning and direction, even while our hearts and minds pull us toward the ever abundant but deceptively arid deserts of modern life. Forgive us, we pray, and shower your quenching Spirit upon us on this latter Pentecost Day, making our own spirits fertile seed-beds for life and growth, for both ourselves and others around us. In the precious name of the Christ we pray. Amen

The Day of Pentecost

Second Lesson: Acts 2:1-21

Theme: God's unifying Spirit

Exegetical note: Luke's account of, in effect, the birthday of the Church at Pentecost, presents the gift of tongues as something different from what Paul would deal with later. Here, actual languages are uttered, which at the same time fulfill prophecy (specifically Joel's) and reverse the effects of the Babel event: language, which once marked human alienation, now becomes a Spirit-given vehicle that overcomes all human estrangement and unifies.

Call to Worship
(based on Psalm 104)

Leader: Without the face of God, we would be dismayed!

People: WITHOUT THE BREATH OF GOD, WE WOULD SURELY DIE!

Leader: Let us look to God for our sustenance!

People: LET US GATHER WITH GLADNESS THE GOOD THINGS GOD GIVES!

Collect

Empowering God, you poured out your Spirit with tongues of fire and produced languages of liberation on that first Pentecost. Bestow upon us today the powerful gift of your presence: that, as human tongues were loosed to declare your glory then, our words may now be free to proclaim your grace. In Jesus' name we pray. Amen

Prayer of Confession

Heavenly God, we confess how much and how often our words serve to manifest and multiply our alienation and estrangement from one another and from you. We speak in self-serving and hateful lies and half-truths; we gossip and gripe; and we criticize and condemn — all because of our condition of sin. Forgive us, we pray, and use your spirit to mend our spirits and cleanse our tongues. Make what we say pure, holy, righteous, and appropriate for those who would be citizens under your coming Reign. In Jesus' name we pray. Amen

The Day of Pentecost

Gospel: John 20:19-23

Theme: God's Spirit of life and forgiveness

Exegetical note: The fact that John here places the giving of the Holy spirit on Easter evening rather than on Pentecost proper should not detract from the central facts that (1) the bestowal of the Spirit as breath recalls God's life-giving creation of Adam in Genesis 2; and (2) the bestowal of the Spirit thus on the apostles is the basis of their mission, which here can be summarized as preaching and baptizing (which is the context for the forgiveness and retention of sins mentioned).

Call to Worship
(based on Psalm 104)

Leader: How manifold are God's works and God's creatures!

People: WITH WHAT WISDOM GOD HAS MADE US ALL!

Leader: God filled the sea with life!

People: GOD RENEWS THE FACE OF THE GROUND!

Collect

Great God, through Jesus you breathed your Holy Spirit on the first disciples, making them apostles of your word to the world. So empower us as well this Pentecost Day: that, filled with your presence as never before, we may carry out a ministry of love and forgiveness and peace. In the name of the Christ we pray. Amen

Prayer of Confession

Most merciful God, we know and admit that as a rule, despite our claims, we are as bereft of your Spirit as empty balloons are of air, and that our souls are deflated and our lives small and earthbound as a result. Forgive us, we pray, and fill us with your warm and buoyant Breath, which raised Adam to life from the clay of the earth, and can lift us to new life from all the worldly cares, concerns, and claims that would pull us and keep us down. In the inspiring name of Jesus we pray. Amen

First Sunday after Pentecost
(The Holy Trinity)

First Lesson: Deuteronomy 4:32-40

Theme: The transcendent, immanent God

Exegetical note: This passage clearly attests the two basic components of Judaeo-Christian theism. For the assertion in v. 39 that God is in heaven and on earth bespeaks both the transcendence of God's being (i.e., God's essential nature prior to, above, beyond, and other than the world) and the immanence of God's activity. That is, the Creator does not become the creation or its creatures (with one notable exception for orthodox Christianity!), but does work redemptively in the world and with its people.

Call to Worship
(based on Psalm 33)

Leader: Let the righteous rejoice in God!

People: FOR GOD'S WORD IS TRUSTWORTHY, AND ALL GOD'S ACTS ARE FAITHFUL!

Leader: God loves righteousness and justice!

People: AND THE EARTH IS FULL OF GOD'S STEADFAST LOVE!

Collect

Almighty God, you were prior to creation and stand above it now as its Holy Other. Convince us again of your abiding care for and presence in the world: that, knowing that you are indeed active in its history and among its people, we may cooperate with you in bringing your majesty and mercy to bear. In Jesus' name we pray. Amen

Prayer of Confession

Most caring Creator, we confess that we sometimes treat you as aloof from the world and far removed from everyday life, for imagining you as distant, we feel free to keep the world at arm's length as well. Forgive us this self-deceit, O God, and assist us in admitting always your continuing concern and compassion for your Creation and creatures. Make the fact that you abide in the world and its affairs move us to involve ourselves graciously as well. In the name of the Christ we pray. Amen

First Sunday after Pentecost
(The Holy Trinity)

Second Lesson: 2 Corinthians 13:5-14

Theme: The Christ-centered Trinity

Exegetical note: The formula that closes the hortatory conclusion to this letter is the only time that Paul explicity refers to the three entities that later became the doctrine of the Trinity for orthodox Christianity. The order that Paul employs here is important (and hardly accidental): Christians experience the grace of the Christ first, and because of that, they experience God's love and the fellowship of the Spirit.

Call to Worship
(based on Psalm 33)

Leader: By God's word were the heavens made!

People: WITH GOD'S BREATH WERE THE WORLD'S CREATURES MADE!

Leader: Let all the earth fear God!

People: LET ALL ITS INHABITANTS STAND IN AWE!

Collect

Holy God, you have shown us your grace in Christ Jesus, and through him your love and the fellowship of the Spirit. Give us now an appreciation of your mysterious threefold nature: that, what we are unable to comprehend, we shall be able to know intuitively because of its impact upon our lives. In the name of the living Christ we pray. Amen

Prayer of Confession

Eternal God, we confess that we often wallow in the incomprehensibility of your majesty, and use the limitations of our human minds as an excuse to ignore you altogether. Forgive us, we pray, and help us to take to heart the saving knowledge of you that an experience of the Christ brings. Let the grace that we have realized in him tell us of your love and lead us to fellowship in your Spirit, to the end that we shall know of you what we need, for both assurance of mind and action in ministry. In Jesus' name we pray. Amen

First Sunday after Pentecost
(The Holy Trinity)

Gospel: Matthew 28:16-20

Theme: The threefold name of God

Exegetical note: Matthew's version of the great commission contained here provides the clearest scriptural statement of the trinitarian formula that would later become the Trinitarian doctrine of orthodox Christianity. Important here is the context given by Jesus for this charge: it is a matter of authority, which has been given to him, and which he, in turn, is passing along to those who will be in mission in the threefold name of God.

Call to Worship
(based on Psalm 33)

Leader: The counsel of God stands forever!

People: THE THOUGHTS OF GOD'S HEART ARE FOR ALL GENERATIONS!

Leader: Blessed are the nations that worship God!

People: BLESSED ARE THE PEOPLES WHOM GOD HAS CHOSEN!

Collect

Triune God, you have given us a threefold name by which to call you and know you. Make it now an inspiration for us: that, knowing you not only as Creator, but Redeemer and Sustainer as well, we may be empowered and enthused to engage in ministry on your behalf and for our sakes. In all of these holy names we pray this day. Amen

Prayer of Confession

Majestic God, we confess that we spend far too much time thinking about you, your Persons, and your Names, and not enough experiencing you in all your fullness. Forgive us, we pray, and open our souls and spirits to the manifold ways in which you can touch us. As Creator, empower us; as Redeemer, save us; and as Sustainer, be with us as we move beyond our limitations of mind to engage in carrying out our missions as your people, your children, your Church. In the name of Jesus we pray. Amen

Proper 4
*Sunday between May 29 and June 4 inclusive
(If after Trinity Sunday)*

First Lesson: Genesis 12:1-9

Theme: Faithful obedience to God's call

Exegetical note: What is most striking about this account of God's call and Abraham's response is the lack of haggling or hesitation on the part of the latter. Rather, Abraham breaks all ties to land and most to family in order to do God's bidding, and thus becomes a model of faithful obedience to God's call for all time.

Call to Worship
(based on Psalm 33)

Leader: Behold, God's eye is upon those who fear God,

People: UPON THOSE WHOSE HOPE IS IN GOD'S STEADFAST LOVE!

Leader: May God deliver us from death!

People: MAY GOD PRESERVE US IN TIMES OF WANT!

Collect

Holy God, you called Abraham to father your people, and us to be your people. Help us to respond in faith as he did: that, obedient to your call, we may be worthy children and effective carriers of your holy word for the world. In the name of Jesus we pray. Amen

Prayer of Confession

Everlasting God, it pains us to confess how unresponsive to your bidding we really are and how faithless to our callings we can be. We do your work, if at all, half-heartedly and act according to your will, at best, when it is convenient for us. Forgive us, we pray, and inspire us with the example of your servants like Abraham, who though they were unworthy and felt unprepared, answered your summons with faith and performed their appointed tasks with grace. In the name of Christ Jesus we pray. Amen

Proper 4
Sunday between May 29 and June 4 inclusive
(If after Trinity Sunday)

Second Lesson: Romans 3:21-28

Theme: True justification versus self-justification

Exegetical note: This selection contains the heart of Paul's theology: (1) all have sinned; (2) God alone is righteous; (3) God manifested that righteousness in Christ Jesus rather than the Law; (4) God justifies believers by grace (a gift) through (5) the redemption/expiation effected. The "bottom line" is that self-justification doesn't work and true justification requires God's agency.

Call to Worship
(based on Psalm 33)

Leader: Let our souls wait upon God!

People: GOD IS OUR HELP AND OUR SHIELD!

Leader: Let our hearts be glad in God!

People: LET US TRUST IN GOD'S HOLY NAME!

Collect

Most holy God, only you are truly righteous and only by your grace in Christ Jesus are we righteous at all. Help us to take to heart the redemption that we have in him: that, the goodness that we were unable to achieve on our own merits, we may by your grace not only realize but reflect. In Jesus' name we pray. Amen

Prayer of Confession

Merciful and loving God, we confess that we often fall into the trap of trying to justify ourselves and to make ourselves righteous on our own merits and by our own efforts; and we admit that, because of our sinfulness, we fail miserably and wind up only feeling more guilty and worthless than before. Forgive us, we pray, and help us to seek and find the only true justification, which you have made available to us in Christ Jesus, and in which alone there is righteousness. In his holy name we pray. Amen

Proper 4
Sunday between May 29 and June 4 inclusive
(If after Trinity Sunday)

Gospel: Matthew 7:21-28

Theme: Lip-service versus true service

Exegetical note: This selection from the Sermon on the Mount gives biblical substantiation to the dictum "deeds not words." For Jesus here contrasts those who pay lip service to God with those who actually do God's will, comparing the former to foolish builders on foundations of sand, and the latter to a wise builder who constructs on a solid base.

Call to Worship

Leader: Blessed are those whose faith is in God!

People: BLESSED ARE THOSE WHO DO GOD'S WILL!

Leader: Blessed are those who build upon the Rock!

People: THEY ARE THE ONES LIFE'S STORMS CANNOT MOVE!

Collect

Eternal God, you have given us in Jesus a firm foundation on which to build our faith. Give us the wisdom to use it: that, rejecting all the unsure ground that the world offers, we may construct by your grace for ourselves and others a building not made with hands: a firm and lasting trust in you. In the name of Jesus we pray. Amen

Prayer of Confession

Almighty God, it shames us to confess how often we play the fool by paying mere lip-service to you, your Christ, and your coming Reign, all the while putting our true allegiance in the world, its standards and its values; and we acknowledge that we always wind up suffering ourselves and bringing shame upon your gospel. Forgive us, we pray, and teach us once and for all that deeds rather than words reveal the true place of the heart and provide the firmest evidence for faith. In the name of Jesus we trust and pray. Amen

Proper 5
Sunday between June 5 and June 11 inclusive
(If after Trinity Sunday)

First Lesson: Genesis 22:1-18

Theme: God will provide

Exegetical note: Behind this well-known story of Abraham's willingness to sacrifice his own son at God's bidding lies a view of God that, for most modern readers, would suggest a measure of insecurity and unreasonableness, if not sadism on the part of the Deity. Be that as it may, in the final analysis, God does provide what is needed in the situation, which (on the basis of vv. 8 and 14) seems to be the real point of the story.

Call to Worship
(based on Psalm 13)

Leader: Let us praise God, who forgets us not!

People: LET US BLESS GOD, WHO HIDES NOT!

Leader: For God in mercy eases our pain!

People: GOD IN GRACE LIFTS OUR SORROW!

Collect

Most holy God, you have provided well for all of your children what was required in all situations. Assist us in accepting your gifts: that, our lives enhanced by your divine blessings, we may lead lives that are more wholesome and holy, and more purposeful and productive. In Jesus' name we pray. Amen

Prayer of Confession

Most loving God, we confess that we do not always trust you to provide for us in all situations, but particularly in times of trouble; and we admit that when you do, we seldom put your wonderful gifts to good use. Forgive us, we pray, and grant us the wisdom to seize and to use all of your blessings, not only to our benefit, but also for the good of others and to the glory of you, your Christ, and your coming Reign. In the name of the Christ we pray. Amen

Proper 5
Sunday between June 5 and June 11 inclusive
(If after Trinity Sunday)

Second Lesson: Romans 4:13-18

Theme: The righteousness of faith

Exegetical note: As Paul continues to expound upon the heart of his own theology, he makes here the point that Abraham is the father (not to mention model) of all true believers. For he was justified by God, not because he earned or merited it through obedience to the Law, but purely and simply because God graciously granted him righteousness, which he in turn trusted. Precisely such trust is Paul's basic definition of "faith."

Call to Worship

Leader: Let us turn our hearts to the worship of God!

People: LET US LIFT OUR VOICES IN THANKS AND PRAISE!

Leader: For God is both righteous and faithful!

People: GOD IS BOTH GRACIOUS AND MERCIFUL!

Collect

Eternal God, you called being out of nothingness and hope out of despair. Teach us to place our faith in you: that, like our forerunners Abraham and Paul, we may trust, not in our own righteousness, but in the bounty of your grace and mercy, by which alone we are justified. In the name of Jesus we pray. Amen

Prayer of Confession

Most patient God, we admit that we place our faith in ourselves and our own abilities and efforts at righteousness far more than we do in you and your grace, and we know that we wind up leading aimless, miserable, and hypocritical lives as a result. Forgive us, we pray, and plant deeply within us a confidence in you and your willingness and ability to transform us out of the abundance of your own righteousness. Make us trustful of your grace and trustworthy of your gospel. In the name of the Christ we pray. Amen

Proper 5
Sunday between June 5 and June 11 inclusive
(If after Trinity Sunday)

Gospel: Matthew 9:9-13

Theme: God's medicine of mercy

Exegetical note: Jesus' association with the despised (here, tax collectors and sinners) and his pronouncements about the need of the sick for a physician and God's desire for mercy all direct the reader's attention to the point that God's interest is not in the self-righteous (who may also be termed "the supposedly-righteous"), but to those who need God's "medicine" of mercy to make them "well."

Call to Worship
(based on Psalm 13)

Leader: Let us trust in God's steadfast love

People: LET OUR HEARTS REJOICE IN GOD'S SALVATION!

Leader: Let us sing to God!

People: FOR GOD HAS DEALT BOUNTIFULLY WITH US!

Collect

Eternal God, you sent us in Christ Jesus a healer with a gospel that was medicine for sin-sick souls. Convince us of our malady: that, recognizing our need for spiritual healing, we may place our trust in that great physician and the wholeness and holiness that only he can bring. In his name we pray. Amen

Prayer of Confession

Most merciful God, we confess that, though we make every effort to give the appearance of spiritual health, our souls in fact are sin-sick; and that, though we take great pains to treat our inner maladies and to cure ourselves, we wind up, at best, self-righteous, which means supposedly-righteous. Forgive us, O God, and grant us a new lease on health and life through the healing powers of your holy gospel of grace, as delivered by him who restored the sick to health and the dead to life. In his holy name we pray. Amen

Proper 6
Sunday between June 12 and June 18 inclusive
(If after Trinity Sunday)

First Lesson: Genesis 25:19-34

Theme: Materialism versus what really matters

Exegetical note: Neither of the principals in this story comes out looking very good: Jacob is portrayed as greedy (albeit clever), and Esau as short-sighted (or downright stupid). Perhaps the best truly timeless lesson here is in the materialism that diverts both from righteousness: Jacob's lust for his brother's rightful double inheritance overcomes both fairness and brotherly love, while Esau's concern to meet immediate physical need (in this case, hunger) clouds his judgment about the future.

Call to Worship
(based on Psalm 46)

Leader: God is our refuge! God is our strength!

People: GOD IS OUR PROVEN HELPER IN TIMES OF TROUBLE!

Leader: Though the mountains quake and the seas roar,

People: YET SHALL WE TRUST IN GOD!

Collect

Creator God, you have warned us often in scripture about the dangers of materialism. Let us hear and heed this word of caution: that, turned away from the distractions of the physical world, we may devote ourselves fully to things of the spirit. In the name of Jesus we pray. Amen

Prayer of Confession

Most generous God, it grieves us to admit just how materialistic we are, how fascinated we are with possessions and playthings, and how short-sighted and downright greedy we are as a result. Forgive us, we pray, and help us to redirect our attention and affections away from the pleasures of earth to the treasures of heaven, from the things that satisfy the physical to those that fulfill the spirit, and from that which is superficial in the present age to that which is substantial in the age to come. In Christ Jesus' holy name we pray. Amen

Proper 6
Sunday between June 12 and June 18 inclusive
(If after Trinity Sunday)

Second Lesson: Romans 5:6-11

Theme: From wretchedness to reconciliation

Exegetical note: Paul's three "while we were (yet)" assertions in this selection underscore the utterly hopeless predicament of humanity before the atoning death of the Christ: helpless, sinners, enemies of God — in other words, completely undeserving of the reconciliation that God effected through that dramatic event. The entire selection may be regarded as an elaboration of the word "wretch" in the second line of the most beloved hymn that calls God's grace, appropriately, "amazing."

Call to Worship
(based on Psalm 46)

Leader: Be still, and know that God is God!

People: LET GOD BE EXALTED AMONG THE NATIONS!

Leader: Let God be exalted in all the earth!

People: FOR THE GOD OF HOSTS IS WITH US; THE GOD OF JACOB IS OUR REFUGE!

Collect

Most holy One, you reconciled us to yourself through Jesus while we were yet sinners. Deal with us graciously now and forever: that, despite our faults and failings, we by your grace may be and remain children of yours and brothers and sisters of the Christ, in whose name we pray. Amen

Prayer of Confession

God of mercy, we confess our utter sinfulness, which resides beneath our many wicked acts within our very natures as a part of our human condition; we recognize the extent to which it has alienated us from you; and we acknowledge our inability to remove it ourselves or to escape its effects. Forgive us, we pray, and touch us again with the grace that we know you have extended to us in the person of Christ Jesus. Cleanse our spirits, purify our actions, and restore us at last to a close relationship with you. In Jesus' name we pray. Amen

Proper 6
Sunday between June 12 and June 18 inclusive
(If after Trinity Sunday)

Gospel: Matthew 9:35—10:8

Theme: The motherly compassion of the Christ

Exegetical note: The verb in verse 35 rendered in English as "had compassion" means literally to have one's "guts" wrenched, vis-a-vis either the bowels or, oddly enough, the womb. What we have on Jesus' part here, then, is the kind of deeply felt, profound love for "harassed and helpless" children usually associated with motherhood, which may well have been its reference in the original Aramaic.

Call to Worship

Leader: As mother's heart aches when a child is harassed and helpless,

People: SO DOES GOD'S COMPASSION EXTEND TO ALL PEOPLE.

Leader: And as a mother's nature is to show mercy upon her children,

People: SO DOES GOD'S LOVING KINDNESS TOUCH US ALL!

Collect

Glorious God, through Jesus you showed your motherly compassion for us, your helpless, hopeless children. Make us now reponsive to your loving kindness: that, touched deeply by your gracious acceptance, we may live as worthy sisters and brothers of Christ Jesus, in whose name we pray. Amen

Prayer of Confession

Gracious God, it humiliates us to admit that, if we are your children, we are mostly problems and prodigals, delinquents and derelicts, and wholly unworthy of being a part of your holy family. We claim your name and that of the Christ, but more often than not we bring shame upon it by our thoughts, our words, and our deeds. Forgive us, O God, and extend to us once again the nurturing warmth of your motherly care, which loves the unlovely, accepts the unacceptable, and brings hope to the hopeless. In Jesus' name we pray. Amen

Proper 7
*Sunday between June 19 and June 25 inclusive
(If after Trinity Sunday)*

First Lesson: Genesis 28:10-17

Theme: The subtle presence of God

Exegetical note: Jacob's response to his dream-theophany — that God had been in that place all along without his knowing it — reflects well the modern-day tendency to let the prevailing secularizing worldview exclude such divine impingement, and yet to have extraordinary events trigger a recognition that the divine presence and power abide, usually *incognito*, even in the midst of everyday life.

Call to Worship
(based on Psalm 91)

Leader: For those who dwell in the shelter of the Most High,

People: OUR GOD IS A MIGHTY FORTRESS!

Leader: For those who dwell in the shadow of the Almighty,

People: OUR GOD IS A SAFE REFUGE!

Collect

Ever-present God, you are with us and within us, among us and around us, even when we do not feel it. Burst through our barriers of insensitivity: that, made thus aware of your abiding presence in our everyday lives, we may live each moment in blessed harmony with you. In the name of Jesus we pray. Amen

Prayer of Confession

Most merciful God, we confess that we have allowed the secularism of modern life to filter you out of our minds, so that we live for the most part without any sense of your presence or power in the world; and we know in our hearts, whenever we stop to think about it, that our lives are faulty and flat, superficial and sad as a result. Forgive us, we pray, and sensitize us once again to the reality of your continuing being and constant abiding in Creation, shaping lives and steering events by the subtle movements of your mighty divine Providence. In the name of your Word made flesh, Christ Jesus, we pray. Amen

Proper 7
Sunday between June 19 and June 25 inclusive
(If after Trinity Sunday)

Second Lesson: Romans 5:12-19

Theme: The "living death" of sin

Exegetical note: Paul's juridical paralleling of Adam and Jesus is one of contrasts: the former's trespass (disobedience) brought condemnation and death to all under the Law; the latter's righteousness (obedience) brought them acquittal and life under grace. The point here is neither to blame Adam for death (see the "because" clause in v. 15) nor to treat physical death as a punishment, but to underscore the "living death" of being estranged from God that everyone's sin (like Adam's) causes.

Call to Worship
(based on Psalm 91)

Leader: Those who trust God fear not the terrors of the night!

People: THOSE WHO LOVE GOD FLEE NOT THE PERILS OF THE DAY!

Leader: For God's grace dispels what stalks the darkness!

People: GOD'S MERCY VANQUISHES THE EVILS OF THE DAY!

Collect

Almighty God, you have rescued us from the living death and eternal damnation that sin would bring us. Impress us again with the magnitude of your grace: that, seeing again the awful end from which you have saved us, we may glory in the freedom and life that you have given us. In Jesus' name we pray. Amen

Prayer of Confession

God of loving kindness, we confess that we live much of our lives as descendents of Adam and heirs to his sin, rather than as brothers and sisters of Jesus and recipients of your grace. Our transgressions are many and our merits are few. Forgive us, we pray, and help us to realign our lives after the image and likeness of the second Adam and his new humanity, so that we may be thus transformed and our lives thus redeemed, to his glory and yours. In his holy name we pray. Amen

Proper 7
Sunday between June 19 and June 25 inclusive
(If after Trinity Sunday)

Gospel: Matthew 10:24-33

Theme: Grounds for Christian courage

Exegetical note: As a part of his parting commission to his disciples, Jesus urges them not to fear on three (rather loosely related) grounds: (1) that what has been hidden (probably the Reign of God proclaimed, often obliquely, by Jesus) will be revealed; (2) that, compared with God's power and providence, nothing is fearsome; and (3) that the faithful will have an advocate in heaven before this God in the person of the Christ.

Call to Worship
(based on Psalm 91)

Leader: Let us worship the God who delivers us from every peril!

People: LET US PRAISE THE GOD WHO PROTECTS US FROM EVERY PLAGUE!

Leader: For God covers us with heavenly wings!

People: GOD DEFENDS US WITH HOLY SHIELDS!

Collect

Mighty God, beside you and your power nothing is fearsome. Grant us the courage required of discipleship: that, trusting in the security of your coming Reign and the support of our advocate Jesus, we may be bold to proclaim the truth of your liberating gospel even to those who would rather not hear. In Jesus' name we pray. Amen

Prayer of Confession

God of the ages, we confess with deep regret our timidity in proclaiming your Word of forgiveness and mercy, grace and hope to the world, because we fear what others will think of us or do to us as a result. We have grown to like our possessions more than our professions, and our comforts more than our commissions as disciples of Christ Jesus. Forgive us, we pray, and adjust our values to conform to your demands rather than to the world's dictates or our desires. In the name of the Christ we pray. Amen

Proper 8
Sunday between June 26 and July 2 inclusive

First Lesson: Genesis 32:22-32

Theme: Wrestling with God

Exegetical note: The identity of Jacob's opponent is uncertain here, both to the patriarch and to the reader. But the names Israel ("he who strives with God") and Peniel ("the face of God") in the story suggest that the "man" with whom he wrestled throughout the night was actually God, and that what we therefore have here dramatized as a physical altercation is an internal, spiritual struggle. The implication is that, even for those with exemplary faith, encounters with God are not always easy.

Call to Worship
(based on Psalm 17)

Leader: May God lend us an ear!

People: MAY GOD HEAR OUR WORDS!

Leader: May our Creator show us steadfast love!

People: MAY OUR REDEEMER GIVE US A GLIMPSE OF GOD'S FACE!

Collect

Most holy God, you have given us in scripture examples of many faithful saints who nevertheless have wrestled with you. Make us willing to engage in such a struggle: that, having contended in faith with you, we may be stronger to face the world as your servants. In the name of Jesus we pray. Amen

Prayer of Confession

God of abundant grace, we confess that, when it comes to matters of faith, we are cowardly and weak, unwilling to engage in the kind of spiritual struggle with doubts and misgivings that in fact strengthens faith and reinforces discipleship. Forgive us our timidity, O God, and set before us the example of all the great saints who, because they were willing to wrestle with you and your angels, as well as with themselves and their passions, were thus empowered as servants of you and disciples of the Christ. In his name we pray. Amen

Proper 8
Sunday between June 26 and July 2 inclusive

Second Lesson: Romans 6:3-11

Theme: Death behind, life ahead

Exegetical note: In this passage Paul suggests a new perspective on death for the Christian on two grounds: (1) first, it is not a future prospect but a thing of the past, since Christians have died with Christ Jesus; and (2) it is not a grim reality, but a positive experience, for it has freed the believers from sin and opened them up to new life. The verb tenses throughout the passage indicate that death is behind, and life is ahead.

Call to Worship

Leader: Let us praise God for allowing us to die to sin!

People: LET US THANK GOD FOR MAKING SIN A THING OF THE PAST!

Leader: Let us worship God, who has given us a new future!

People: LET US GLORIFY GOD, WHO HAS GIVEN US NEW LIFE!

Collect

Great Spirit God, you have placed death behind us and life before us in Christ Jesus. Help us now to live accordingly: that, as ones resurrected by your grace, we may renew the world and revitalize its people with your holy gospel. In the name and spirit of Jesus we pray. Amen

Prayer of Confession

Most understanding God, we confess that we live in mortal fear of death, even while we do the very things that sow death in our lives and the lives of others, and that even threaten to bring death upon the entire planet. We use our minds to destructive ends, and we live thoughtlessly for the moment, with little regard for the long-range fatal effects of our actions. Forgive us, we pray, and make us truly a people for whom death is a thing of the past, defeated in the resurrection of Jesus, and driven completely from your coming Reign. In Jesus' holy name we pray. Amen

Proper 8
Sunday between June 26 and July 2 inclusive

Gospel: Matthew 10:34-42

Theme: The downside of discipleship

Exegetical note: As he concludes his commissioning and instructing of his disciples, Jesus here issues a caveat: all will not be "sweetness and light" for them. Discipleship will require sacrifices (including familial relationships) and sufferings (including crosses), and even losses of life — which, paradoxically, will mean the finding of (new) life. In other words, the life of the Christian will be modeled after the life of the Christ, hardships and all.

Call to Worship

Leader: Let us rejoice to be in God's house!

People: LET US BE JOYFUL TO ENTER GOD'S SANCTUARY!

Leader: Let us be glad to approach God's throne!

People: LET US EXULT TO BEHOLD GOD'S FACE AND TO UTTER GOD'S NAME!

Collect

God of truth, you have warned us well that Christian discipleship will not be easy. Give us the courage to face its hardships: that, reinforced for the sacrifices that following Jesus must bring, we shall be effective servants and bold conveyors of your gracious Word for the world. In Jesus' name we pray. Amen

Prayer of Confession

God of tenderness, we are sad to say how much we have made Christian discipleship a way of comfort and ease rather than one of challenge and exertion. We have abandoned any notion of sacrifice, and put out of our minds any thought of crosses that might have to be borne or costs that might need to be paid. Forgive us, O God, and set before us again both the words and the way of Christ Jesus. Make us bold to accept willingly and to embrace gladly whatever hardships may come as we seek and strive to serve you. In the name of the Suffering Servant, Jesus, we pray. Amen

Proper 9
Sunday between July 3 and July 9 inclusive

First Lesson: Exodus 1:6-14, 22—2:10

Theme: Godly civil disobedience

Exegetical note: The story of the Pharoah's ineffective plot to decimate the burgeoning Hebrew population by killing its newborn males is a tale of the godliness, courage, and cleverness of a series of "powerless" women in the face of abused political authority. The omitted verses here (15-21) tell of first the Jewish midwives who refuse to cooperate. Then Moses' mother and sister conspire successfully to save him. Even Pharoah's daughter, out of sheer human compassion, knowingly defies her father's cruel orders.

Call to Worship
(based on Psalm 124)

Leader: If God had not been on Israel's side,

People: THEIR ENEMIES WOULD HAVE SWALLOWED THEM UP ALIVE!

Leader: If God likewise were not our strength,

People: THEN THE FLOODS OF LIFE WOULD WASH US AWAY!

Collect

Most righteous God, you have given us many examples of saints who have disobeyed earthly rulers and rules for godly reasons. Give us also such courage: that, not weighing the personal risk, we may be ready to fight injustice and inhumanity wherever they exist. In Jesus' name we pray. Amen

Prayer of Confession

Loving God, we confess that we have time and again turned our attention from injustice in the world, and have either pretended that it didn't exist, or told ourselves that it wasn't our fault or our place to fight it. Forgive us, O God, and remind us with the example of Jesus that an important part of the Christian life is the kind of compassion that cannot stand to see people suffering unfairly, and that fights even powers and principalities to oppose oppression and end inequity. In the name of Jesus we pray. Amen

Proper 9
Sunday between July 3 and July 9 inclusive

Second Lesson: Romans 7:14-25a

Theme: The overwhelming power of sin

Exegetical note: Paul's personal confession of his own powerlessness in the face of sin contains a deep psychological insight about the overwhelming power of sin and every human's inevitable struggle with it. For sin is a problem not just for the malicious evildoers "out there somewhere." On the contrary, even the godly with the best of intentions find themselves acting against their own wills and minds (v. 25b).

Call to Worship
(based on Psalm 124)

Leader: Blessed be God, for not giving us over to sin!

People: WITH GOD'S HELP, WE HAVE ESCAPED LIKE BIRDS FROM A SNARE!

Leader: In Christ, the snare is broken, and we are set free!

People: OUR HELP IS IN GOD, WHO MADE HEAVEN AND EARTH!

Collect

Eternal God, you have recognized the overwhelming power of sin in our lives and have overcome it in the person of Jesus. Bring your mercy to bear on us: that, touched by your exceeding grace, we may gain control over every evil that would separate us from you. In the name of the Christ we pray. Amen

Prayer of Confession

Merciful God, we confess that, like Paul before us, we stand powerless in the face of sin, and wind up doing the evil that we want to resist, and not doing the good that we know we should. We have tried to resist the Satan in our hearts, and have failed miserably. Forgive us, we pray; touch us with the redeeming power of your love; and fill us with your sustaining Spirit. For only by your grace can we be free to become the children of light that you would have us be. In the name of Jesus we pray. Amen

Proper 9
Sunday between July 3 and July 9 inclusive

Gospel: Matthew 11:25-30

Theme: The bearable lightness of grace

Exegetical note: The specific meaning of verse 28, which is often used out of context as a word of comfort at funerals, is revealed by the following verses, which refer to a "yoke." In Jesus' day, the Law was referred to as a yoke, because it was demanding and burdensome. (The Hindu tradition also called its basic spiritual discipline *yoga*, Sanskrit for "yoke"!) By contrast, says Jesus, his message is "easy" and his "burden is light." For it rests, not upon human obedience, but upon God's grace.

Call to Worship

Leader: Let us open our eyes to God's glory!

People: LET US OPEN OUR EARS TO GOD'S WORD!

Leader: Let us open our minds to God's gospel of grace!

People: LET US OPEN OUR HEARTS TO GOD'S LOVE!

Collect

Heavenly God, you removed from us the burden of the Law and touched us lightly with your grace. Lift sin completely from us: that, freed from its unbearable weight, we may stand tall and walk with ease in the your paths of righteousness. In Jesus' name we pray. Amen

Prayer of Confession

God of tender mercy, we sadly confess that the reality of your grace and mercy often escapes us, and that we frequently find ourselves still trying to win your love by our merits and to secure salvation by our own feeble efforts, instead of trusting in you and your love in Christ Jesus. Forgive us, we pray, and convince us once and for all that our loads have been lifted and our burdens made light by the atoning work of the one we call the Lamb. In his redeeming name we pray. Amen

Proper 10
Sunday between July 10 and July 16 inclusive

First Lesson: Exodus 2:11-22

Theme: God's unlikely candidates

Exegetical note: Moses' troubling lack of hesitation or remorse over his act of murder aside, the real point of that incident, as well as of his assistance of and sojourn with the Midianites, seems to be his rootlessness and lack of identity before his call: he is born Hebrew, but reared Egyptian; exiled from Egypt because of his passionate defense of his true people, but then adopted a second time by the Midianites, though regarded by them as an Egyptian. The picture is of a man with a very unstable background, an unlikely candidate for God's call.

Call to Worship

Leader: Let us worship the God of Israel!

People: LET US PRAISE THE GOD WHO CALLED HIM TO SERVE!

Leader: Let us give thanks to the God who looks past our human frailties!

People: LET US ADORE THE GOD WHO KNOWS OUR HEARTS AND FREES OUR SPIRITS!

Collect

Holy God, you have time and again taken rootless people with no identity and made them effective servants of you and your will. Do likewise with us: that, despite our faults and limitations, we may become and remain instruments of your grace. In Jesus' name we pray. Amen

Prayer of Confession

God of boundless love, we confess that we use our humble stations in life and our limited talents as excuses to avoid serving you. We ignore your call and watch and wait for more visible saints to do your work. Forgive us, O God, and set before us the biblical examples of unlikely candidates for service to you, who, despite their handicaps and often their objections, yet by your power became movers and shakers for righteousness and justice, mercy and peace. In the name of Christ Jesus we pray. Amen

Proper 10
Sunday between July 10 and July 16 inclusive

Second Lesson: Romans 8:9-17

Theme: Not slaves or debtors, but sons (and daughters!)

Exegetical note: Though there is still some disagreement about the extent of Hellenistic dualism in Paul's thought, it seems prudent not to read him in a too Neoplatonistic (dualistic) light, but rather to view his references to "flesh" and "spirit" as both referring humans in a more holistic sense, the former meaning their unredeemed state and the latter their redeemed. Whereas "fleshly humans" are captives and debtors, "spiritual humans" are sons and daughters, who can therefore call God "Abba," or "Dad."

Call to Worship

Leader: Rejoice, Christians, for you are captives no more!

People: HALLELUJAH, FOR WE ARE FREED FROM SIN!

Leader: Praise God, whose Spirit makes us debtors no longer!

People: THANKS BE FOR THE CHRIST, THROUGH WHOM WE ARE MADE CHILDREN OF GOD!

Collect

Eternal God, in Christ you have turned slaves and debtors to Satan into sons and daughters of yours. Make this fact a reality for us: that, freed from sin, we may truly join your holy family as brothers and sisters of Christ Jesus, in whose name we pray. Amen

Prayer of Confession

Most holy God, it is difficult for us to admit to you and ourselves just how unredeemed our lives still feel despite your gracious and merciful action toward us in Christ Jesus. Instead of acting like the sons and daughters of God that you have made us, we still often behave as slaves and captives of Satan, being unrighteous and doing evil. Forgive us, we pray, and remove from us every tendency and temptation to sin. Remake us in the image of your perfect Child, in whose name we pray. Amen

Proper 10
Sunday between July 10 and July 16 inclusive

Gospel: Matthew 13:1-9, 18-23

Theme: Facing failures with the gospel proclamation

Exegetical note: The main point of the original parable (vv. 1-9), rather than the almost certainly later allegorical interpretation of the Church (vv. 18ff.), seems to be that, despite the fact that eventually it will find a fertile audience and yield extraordinary fruit, the gospel will initially and repeatedly fail to take root. In this regard, the injunction in verse 9 is telling the hearers of the parable either to heed its lesson, or simply to let the gospel itself "fall on deaf ears," if need be.

Call to Worship

Leader: May God make us fertile soil for the gospel!

People: MAY GOD MAKE US DILIGENT SOWERS OF THE WORD!

Leader: May God grant us the patience to endure failure!

People: MAY GOD GIVE US THE FAITH TO EXPECT A RICH HARVEST!

Collect

Great God, you have given us a gospel to spread and a warning that it may fall on deaf ears. Give us now patience: that, despite the apparent failure of our message to take root, we may yet proclaim it in confidence that the seeds of your Word are being planted. In Jesus' name we pray. Amen

Prayer of Confession

Most holy God, we confess that we are easily discouraged in the performance of your work, and particularly in the task of proclaiming your gospel of love and mercy to the world. We see few visible results and take that as an excuse to shirk our responsibility to your holy Word. Forgive us, we pray, and inspire us again with the parable of the sower. Let us not be discouraged with the seemingly barren or rocky soil, but certain of the power of your holy seed to find fertile ground. In the name of the Christ we pray. Amen

Proper 11
Sunday between July 17 and July 23 inclusive

First Lesson: Exodus 3:1-12

Theme: The majesty and mystery of God

Exegetical note: God's call to Moses in the presence of the burning bush is a classic theophany, presenting the Holy as what Rudolf Otto called a *mysterium tremendum et fascinans* (i.e., a mystery that is both terrifying and magnetic): on the one hand, Moses is drawn to the burning bush and has to be warned not to go near; on the other, he is afraid to look at God and hides his face. The whole incident, therefore, bespeaks the majesty and the mystery of God that leaves humans awestruck and wanting more.

Call to Worship
(based on Psalm 103)

Leader: Let all that is within us bless God's holy name!

People: LET US REMEMBER GOD'S BENEFITS IN OUR VERY SOULS!

Leader: For God forgives and heals and redeems!

People: GOD IS LOVING AND MERCIFUL AND GOOD!

Collect

Most awesome God, you have revealed yourself in majestic mystery to your faithful servants. Give us now a glimpse of your divinity: that, beholding your wondrous glory, we may depart newly inspired to serve you. In the name of Jesus we pray. Amen

Prayer of Confession

Most grand and glorious God, we confess our tendency to reduce you in our minds to a merely superhuman being rather than Being Itself, and to deal with you as "the Man Upstairs" rather than the majestic and mysterious God of power and might that you are. Forgive us, we pray, and teach us by the example of your encounter with Moses in the burning bush that, even while drawn to you as Friend, we mere mortals must approach your cosmic presence with awe and wonder, fear and trembling, reverence and respect. In the name of Christ Jesus we pray. Amen

Proper 11
Sunday between July 17 and July 23 inclusive

Second Lesson: Romans 8:18-25

Theme: Sin as earth-shaking

Exegetical note: Though a literal reading of Genesis 3 is untenable to the modern scientific worldview (and contemporary exegesis!), the notion of the world itself "groaning" because of Adam's original disobedience does point to the far-reaching, earth-shaking effects of human sin that belie our tendency to individualize the human plight and its remedy through the gospel. One need only think of our potentially catastrophic pollution or the potential devastation of a nuclear holocaust to see the truth in Paul's image.

Call to Worship
(based on Psalm 103)

Leader: God is merciful and gracious!

People: GOD ABOUNDS IN STEADFAST LOVE!

Leader: God does not deal with us according to our sins!

People: GOD TREATS US WITH THE COMPASSIONATE KINDNESS OF A LOVING PARENT!

Collect

Creator God, you have given us a world full of wonderful treasures. Teach us to treat it wisely: that, using its resources to promote life, we may overcome all of the negative effects of sin that threaten to destroy the earth and its creatures. In Jesus' name we pray. Amen

Prayer of Confession

Most gracious God, we know that we consistently underestimate the power of sin and ignore the catastrophic effects that it has had on the world and its inhabitants. We misuse the earth's resources in wasteful and harmful ways; we pollute its winds and waters with the by-products of our squander; and we harvest and mine its valuable resources only to fashion objects of vanity or weapons of annihilation. Forgive us, great God, and teach us to be better guardians and stewards of that over which you have given us dominion. In the name of Jesus we pray. Amen

Proper 11
Sunday between July 17 and July 23 inclusive

Gospel: Matthew 13:24-30, 36-43

Theme: God's discrimination

Exegetical note: One of the most disturbing slogans to come out of America's recent war experiences was "Kill them all, and let God sort them out!" The parable of the tares (or "weeds") offers a much more positive angle on divine discrimination, both in its original form (vv. 24-30) and in its (almost certainly later) allegorical interpretation (vv. 36-43). The suggestion is that in God's Reign (and in the Church) no artificial human "weeding" is necessary: "Save them all, and let God sort them out!"

Call to Worship
(based on Psalm 103)

Leader: Let all the angels and heavenly hosts bless God,

People: AND ALL WHO ENDEAVOR TO DO GOD'S WORD AND WILL!

Leader: Let all the works of creation bless God,

People: IN EVERY CORNER OF GOD'S HOLY REIGN!

Collect

Glorious God, you have given us a gospel directed to all humanity. Give us now the vision and scope to match it: that, empowered with a measure of your universal love, we shall not rest until all humanity finds peace in you and your coming Reign. In the name and spirit of the Christ we pray. Amen

Prayer of Confession

Most merciful God, we admit with a deep sense of shame our tendency to be selective in our sharing of the gospel, and to pick and choose those with whom we share the good news of your mercy and forgiveness, both in word and in deed. Forgive us our narrowness of mind and smallness of heart, we pray, and fill us with your Spirit of universal love and grace. Make us determined disciples and able apostles, whose mission to the world has no boundaries, and whose message to humankind has no limits. In Jesus' name we pray. Amen

July 29, 1990

Proper 12
Sunday between July 24 and July 30 inclusive

First Lesson: Exodus 3:13-20

Theme: The God of action

Exegetical note: God's revelation of the divine name, YHWH (or JHWH or JeHoWaH) to Moses is almost a tease. The basis of the name is "to be," but is so ambiguous in form that it may mean "I am who I am," "I will be what I will be," or "He causes to be." The first two of these suggest a more Greek, philosophical, abstract "Being," an appropriate object of speculation. The third seems more Hebraic, for it bespeaks activity and action, which is exactly what God promises (and delivers!) on behalf of the captive Israelites.

Call to Worship
(based on Psalm 105)

Leader: Give thanks to God! Call upon God's name!

People: MAKE KNOWN GOD'S DEEDS TO ALL PEOPLES!

Leader: Sing praises to God! Tell of God's works!

People: GLORY AND REJOICE IN GOD'S NAME!

Collect

God of providence and action, you have brought into being all that is. Move among us now in creative ways: that, touched by your divine presence, we also may become agents of your redemptive grace. In the name of Christ Jesus we pray. Amen

Prayer of Confession

God of promise and assurance, we confess that we are prone to turn you into a mere premise or abstraction, an object of thought and speculation, or a mere element in a formula for explaining whatever puzzles us about the universe or life. Forgive us, we pray, and remind us again that you are a God, not just of dynamic being in nature, but of redemptive action in history, at work in your creation for the well-being of all of your creatures. In Jesus' name we pray. Amen

Proper 12
Sunday between July 24 and July 30 inclusive

Second Lesson: Romans 8:26-30

Theme: A sighing Spirit for dumbfounded saints

Exegetical note: The picture of the Spirit presented in the first two verses here is a powerful one, best illustrated by the defense-advocate in the courtroom, who speaks on behalf of a helpless client. The latter here are saints who are dumbfounded by their weakness (i.e., sin), and who therefore require the kind of profound intercession before God that only God's Spirit itself can provide, and that in unspeakable sighs!

Call to Worship
(based on Psalm 105)

Leader: Seek God and God's strength!

People: SEEK GOD'S PRESENCE WITHOUT CEASING!

Leader: Remember God's wonderful works!

People: REMEMBER GOD'S EVERLASTING WORDS!

Collect

Most benevolent God, you have provided your Spirit as an able spokesperson for a humanity dumbfounded by sin. Continue to stand by us: that, despite our guilt at failing to meet the demands of your Law, your gracious advocacy will acquit us in the high court of your holy justice. In the name of the Christ we pray. Amen

Prayer of Confession

Most gracious God, we confess that we consistently try to justify ourselves with explanations, excuses, rationalizations, and other empty words of self-justification, when in fact we know that we are guilty of sin and deserving of your divine retribution. Forgive us, we pray, and teach us to rely upon the advocacy of your own Holy Spirit, whose gracious intercession alone can bring us unmerited righteousness and undeserved release. In the precious name of Jesus we pray. Amen

Proper 12

Sunday between July 24 and July 30 inclusive

Gospel: Matthew 13:44-52

Theme: A Reign worth any sacrifice

Exegetical note: The first two parables in this selection form a pair and say essentially the same thing from two perspectives: God's coming Reign is like a treasure or rare jewel that is so invaluable that it is worth total sacrifice. Matthew's message in recording these two parables was probably an indirect exhortation to his contemporary Church to accept self-sacrifice willingly.

Call to Worship

Leader: Let us worship the God of hidden treasures!

People: LET US PRAISE THE GOD OF UNTOLD RICHES!

Leader: Let us pledge ourselves to seek God's coming Reign!

People: LET US SACRIFICE ALL FOR A PORTION OF GOD'S PROMISED BLESSINGS!

Collect

Holy God, you have promised us in scripture a coming Reign more precious than a buried treasure. Convince us of its exceeding value: that, forsaking the desire for the false riches of this world, we may willingly sacrifice all to possess your gracious gift. In Jesus' name we pray. Amen

Prayer of Confession

Most compassionate God, we confess our attraction to the earthly treasures that please the flesh for a while, but pass and fade away, and to ignore the promised riches of your coming Reign, whose value is limitless and whose worth is beyond comparison. Forgive us, we pray, and alter our desires and attachments by the power of your Spirit. Make us long for the timeless spiritual wealth that you so graciously have offered us, before which the possessions of this world pale, and for which we should be willing to pay any price, were it not so freely given. In the name of Christ Jesus we pray. Amen

Proper 13
Sunday between July 31 and August 6 inclusive

First Lesson: Exodus 12:1-14

Theme: Trusting God's promises

Exegetical note: Despite its centrality in the history of the Jewish people, the story of the Passover has some troubling aspects, not the least of which is the image of a God who would strike down the first-born — presumably including some children — of any nation. The most useful image here, therefore, may be that in verse 11: so certain are the Israelites of God's acting in their behalf, they eat clothed for the promised journey.

Call to Worship
(based on Psalm 143)

Leader: May God hear our prayers!

People: MAY GOD HEED OUR SUPPLICATIONS!

Leader: May God answer us in faithfulness!

People: MAY GOD BLESS US IN RIGHTEOUSNESS!

Collect

Most trustworthy God, you have always stood by your people and kept your promises. Help us to deepen our faith in you: that, firmly convinced of your dependability, we may live in expectation of your many mercies and abiding presence. In Jesus' name we pray. Amen

Prayer of Confession

Most patient God, we confess that we do not live lives of true faith, believing that the good things that you have promised will come to pass, but rather lower our expectations and qualify our trust, and wind up relying upon ourselves and our own abilities rather than upon your power and providence. Forgive us, we pray, and cultivate within us by your Holy Spirit the conviction that you are as good as your word, that you will be active in our lives in redemptive ways, and that you will be our constant companion and helper on life's journey. In the name of Jesus we pray. Amen

Proper 13
Sunday between July 31 and August 6 inclusive

Second Lesson: Romans 8:31-39

Theme: The unassailable power of God's love

Exegetical note: Paul here paints God as the perfect ally, under whose protection (i.e., justification) the Christian is invincible. The reason for this confidence, it seems, is the power of God's love for humanity in the Christ, which none of the formidable "enemies" enumerated in vv. 38f. can begin to assail, including death!

Call to Worship
(based on Psalm 143)

Leader: May God deliver us from our enemies!

People: MAY GOD BE OUR EVER-PRESENT REFUGE!

Leader: When we are threatened with destruction and our spirits are faint,

People: MAY GOD PRESERVE US WITH STEADFAST LOVE!

Collect

Almighty God, you have shown to us the power of your love in the person of Jesus. Continue as our ally: that, fortified by the strength of your presence, we may resist every enemy that life sends our way, even death. In the name of the victorious Christ we pray. Amen

Prayer of Confession

Most gracious and loving God, we admit with regret our tendency to try to "go it alone" in life, and to face its challenges and catastrophes, its troubles and trials, and its hardships and horrors with only our own limited strength to see us through. Forgive us, we pray, and convince us again of the unassailable power of your love, which alone can face even the threat of death. Be and remain our ally in all of the struggles of life, and make us victors at last after the example of the Christ, in whose name we pray. Amen

Proper 13
Sunday between July 31 and August 6 inclusive

Gospel: Matthew 14:13-21

Theme: The miraculous power of love

Exegetical note: Though it is extremely difficult to try to get behind the narrative accounts of Jesus' miracles to what "really" happened, an interesting possibility has recently been suggested that both fits with the style of Jesus' ministry *and* preserves the miraculous side of this particular event: perhaps what is preserved here (with later eucharistic and fantastic overtones) is an authentic miracle of sharing on the crowd's part, instigated by Jesus' example. The incident, then, becomes a lesson in the miraculous power of love.

Call to Worship

Leader: Sisters and brothers, ours is a God of power!

People: IF GOD IS FOR US, WHO CAN OPPOSE US?

Leader: But this God of power is also a God of love!

People: AND FROM THAT LOVE, NOT EVEN DEATH CAN SEPARATE US!

Collect

Creator God, you have demonstrated to us the miraculous power of love in the life and ministry of Jesus. Fill us now with this divine gift: that, reinforced by its tender might, we may become agents of your mercy and bearers of your grace. In the name of Jesus we pray. Amen

Prayer of Confession

Compassionate God, it hurts us deeply to confess how fond we are of the many kinds of earthly power, particularly wealth and politics; to admit how admiring we are of those who are powerful on those terms; and to recognize how little we avail ourselves of your heavenly power of love, which can move the mightiest of mountains and the heaviest of hearts. Forgive us, we pray, and teach us to abandon the empty promises and short-term gains of the merely human for the trustworthy claims and eternal rewards that are truly divine. In Jesus' name we pray. Amen

Proper 14
Sunday between August 7 and August 13 inclusive

First Lesson: Exodus 14:19-31

Theme: God's safe-keeping Spirit

Exegetical note: Although Paul made the crossing of the Red Sea a type for Christian baptism (1 Corinthians 10:1-2), the incident would seem to have much broader implications: God's miraculous rescue of the Israelites from their "deep waters" (both literal and figurative) prefigures God's removal of all believers from whatever "deep waters" they find themselves confronting. Noteworthy here, of course, is the suggestion (v. 21) that God actually worked through a natural phenomenon, notably wind (cf. "breath," "spirit").

Call to Worship
(Psalm 106)

Leader: Give thanks to God! For God is good!

People: GOD'S STEADFAST LOVE ENDURES FOREVER!

Leader: No one can utter God's mighty works!

People: NO TONGUE CAN TELL THE WONDER OF GOD'S WONDROUS ACTS!

Collect

Almighty God, you have always rescued your people from whatever deep waters they encountered. Make us sensitive to the subtle movements of your Spirit: that, even in the seemingly natural events around us, we may see your redemptive handiwork. In the name of Jesus we pray. Amen

Prayer of Confession

Loving God of mercy, we confess that whenever we encounter "deep waters" in the course of our lives, our first impulse is to deal with them under our own power and relying upon our own abilities; and we admit that, more often than not, we wind up "over our heads." Forgive us, we pray, and remind us with the example of the Israelites at the Red Sea that you will be active on our behalf to overcome whatever obstacles we encounter, however insurmountable they may seem. In Jesus' name we pray. Amen

Proper 14
Sunday between August 7 and August 13 inclusive

Second Lesson: Romans 9:1-5

Theme: The apostasy of the advantaged

Exegetical note: Paul's heart-felt expression of "anguish" and "sorrow" for his fellow Jews over their rejection of the Christ in spite of their many advantages (enumerated in v. 4) may well be universalized to include those of every age and place who, despite their God-given advantages, yet reject God's most exceptional acts of grace and mercy.

Call to Worship

Leader: Sisters and brothers, let us worship the God of Israel!

People: LET US LIFT OUR VOICES TO THE GOD OF ABRAHAM, ISAAC AND JACOB!

Leader: Let us exalt the God of Moses and David!

People: MAY THE GOD OF CHRIST JESUS BE BLESSED FOR EVER!

Collect

Glorious God, you have given us advantages and blessings beyond number. Help us to keep these in proper perspective: that, looking beyond the gifts to the Giver, we make of them opportunities rather than obstacles for faith and righteousness. In the name of the Christ we pray. Amen

Prayer of Confession

God of infinite forgiveness, we confess that we often allow our many advantages — of power, position, prestige and possessions — to become obstacles of faithful service to you. Indeed, we often find ourselves so in bondage to such things that true ministry to others in your name becomes difficult if not impossible. Forgive us, we pray, and help us to use whatever favorable status we have as an occasion for furthering your precious gospel and building your coming Reign upon the earth. In Jesus' name we pray. Amen

Proper 14
Sunday between August 7 and August 13 inclusive

Gospel: Matthew 14:22-33

Theme: The power of faith

Exegetical note: Matthew's reworking of Mark's earlier story shows embellishment of detail and a special "spin" that makes it an allegory of the Church (i.e., boat) in his day, which was being "beaten" by the "stormy seas" of persecution. The story is both a testimony to the power of faith to permit believers to "tread upon the waters" of threatening, fearsome circumstances, and (if faith falters) a reassuring promise of Jesus' "rescuing" hand.

Call to Worship
(based on Psalm 106)

Leader: Blessed are those who do justice!

People: BLESSED ARE THOSE WHO ARE ALWAYS RIGHTEOUS!

Leader: May God show us favor!

People: MAY GOD DELIVER US!

Collect

Eternal God, you have mercifully thrown a drowning humanity the life-line of faith in the person of the Christ. Give us now the power and will to grasp it tightly: that, life's stormy seas notwithstanding, we shall be rescued and saved by your grace. In Jesus' name we pray. Amen

Prayer of Confession

Ever-living God, we confess that our faith, like Peter's, falters and fails at all the worst times, and that, like him, we find ourselves sinking in life's deep waters and stormy seas as a result of the timidity of our faith. Forgive our weakness of heart and spirit, O God, and remind us that, when all else fails, we shall still find ourselves in the grasp of the saving hand of Christ Jesus, whose love and compassion never fail. In his holy name we humbly pray. Amen

Proper 15
Sunday between August 14 and August 20 inclusive

First Lesson: Exodus 16:2-15

Theme: Murmuring against God

Exegetical note: The reaction of the wandering Israelites to their new-found freedom from captivity was almost predictably human: the grass, it seems, had been greener in Egypt than it was now in the desert. Specifically, they were hungry, and "murmured" against God, who responded, not vindictively, but graciously by providing food morning and evening.

Call to Worship
(based on Psalm 78)

Leader: May the God of Moses be with us this hour!

People: MAY THE GOD WHO DELIVERED ISRAEL FROM BONDAGE BE WITH US THIS DAY!

Leader: For ours is a God who liberates!

People: OURS IS A GOD WHO PROVIDES!

Collect

Most gracious God, you have borne the discontent and murmurings of your people throughout history. Continue to be patient with us: that, despite our complaints, we may find ourselves, as always, recipients of your grace and all your many blessings. In Jesus' name we pray. Amen

Prayer of Confession

Most patient God, we confess that we love to complain about our lots in life, the seeming injustices we suffer, and most any little hassle we experience, and to ignore the many benefits and blessings, graces and gifts that we continually receive from the rich bounty of your love. Forgive us our attitudes, O God; soothe our troubled minds and souls by the sustaining presence of your Holy Spirit; and soften our hearts, so that we shall be moved to share the wonderful things we have, rather than to complain about what we think we lack. In the name of Jesus we pray. Amen

Proper 15
Sunday between August 14 and August 20 inclusive

Second Lesson: Romans 11:13-16, 29-32

Theme: God's irrevocable grace

Exegetical note: Paul's deep concern for his fellow Jews finds expression here in the now seemingly desperate hope that somehow their rejection of the gospel has worked to make it more attractive to Gentiles, whose acceptance of it in turn will make the Jews jealous and lead some, at least, finally to it. By far the most timeless declaration is in v. 29, to the effect that God's gifts and call are irrevocable.

Call to Worship

Leader: Let us worship the God whose covenants are forever!

People: LET US WORSHIP THE GOD WHOSE LOVE IS EVERLASTING!

Leader: For the grace of God is irrevocable!

People: AND THE CALL OF GOD IS FOR ALL TIME!

Collect

Most dependable God, you have placed upon us a calling and have bestowed upon us gifts that no one can take away. Endow us now with a sense of purpose: that, knowing our vocation and realizing your assistance, we may engage in ministry and mission in the name of the Christ. In his name we pray. Amen

Prayer of Confession

Most understanding God, we confess that we regularly and thoroughly forget, ignore, or refuse both our calling to be your servants and the gifts that you have provided for that task; and that we spend far more time with our own vocations and labors, and even avocations and leisures, than we ever do on the work of your Christ and coming Reign. Forgive us, we pray, and help us at last to take seriously your summons to ministry and your provisions for that task. Make us finally as constant in our Christian profession as you are in the fulfillment of your promises. In Jesus' name we pray. Amen

Proper 15
Sunday between August 14 and August 20 inclusive

Gospel: Matthew 15:21-28

Theme: Faith that overcomes obstacles

Exegetical note: Matthew's designation of the woman in this passage as a Canaanite (and thus a traditional enemy to the Jews) reveals his intention (in contrast to Mark's) to make this incident speak to the place of Gentiles with respect to the gospel in a most dramatic way. Despite Jesus' insistence (v. 24) that his mission is only to Jews, he is "won over" by her faith and works the miracle of exorcism on her daughter that she has requested.

Call to Worship

Leader: Children of God, let us worship in spirit and truth!

People: LET US WORSHIP IN WORD AND IN SONG!

Leader: For we are in the house of the God of Israel!

People: WE ARE IN THE TEMPLE OF THE GOD OF ALL HUMANKIND!

Collect

Universal God, you have given us a gospel for all humanity. Remove from our hearts and minds all obstacles: that, freed from our prejudices and biases, we may have the kind of faith that will overcome all that would prevent our participation in your coming Reign. In Jesus' name we pray. Amen

Prayer of Confession

Eternal God, it is painful for us to admit just how much we let all sorts of considerations of age, gender, nationality, and race stand in the way of our sharing our faith with our fellow humanity, and how far we thus fall short of realizing the universality of your gospel in Christ Jesus. Forgive us, we pray, and overcome our prejudices and biases, which serve only as obstacles to your gracious message of love and mercy for the world. In the name of Jesus and the spirit of his boundless love we pray. Amen

Proper 16
Sunday between August 21 and August 27 inclusive

First Lesson: Exodus 17:1-7

Theme: The apparent absence of God

Exegetical note: At first it appears that the thirsty (and by now weary) Israelites are expressing merely a pressing physical need and resulting discontent with their leader, but that Moses inflates their complaint to include God. Verse 7, however, suggests that the people's complaint had indeed included God. Their question stemmed from the apparent absence of God in a time of crisis.

Call to Worship
(based on Psalm 95)

Leader: Come, let us sing unto God!

People: LET US MAKE A JOYFUL NOISE TO THE ROCK OF OUR SALVATION!

Leader: Let us come into God's presence with thanksgiving!

People: LET US RAISE TO GOD SONGS OF PRAISE!

Collect

Eternal God, you were with the Israelites in the wilderness, even when they could not feel your presence. Be with us as well: that, knowing that you are near, we may endure every crisis and desert place that we experience in our own life-journeys. In the name of Jesus we pray. Amen

Prayer of Confession

Ever-present God, we confess how similar we are to the wandering Israelites of old in our tendency to conclude and complain, in the face of the least little crisis or physical need, that you are absent. Forgive us, we pray, and sensitize us to the subtleties of your abiding presence and ongoing providence. Reassure us always that you are near, helping us, blessing us, healing us, and benefiting us, even when we are too self-centered and insensitive to realize it. In the name of Jesus we trust and pray. Amen

September 9, 1990

Proper 16
Sunday between August 21 and August 27 inclusive

Second Lesson: Romans 11:33-36

Theme: Wonder before the wisdom of God

Exegetical note: Having finished his discourse on Israel's role of disobedience in the history of salvation, Paul issues this doxology, which focuses on the inscrutable wisdom of God, which makes God the source of all things and thus can only inspire wonder and awe, humility and respect among mere mortals.

Call to Worship
(based on Psalm 95)

Leader: Let us worship the God who is above all gods!

People: FOR IN GOD'S HANDS ARE THE DEPTHS OF THE EARTH!

Leader: The heights of the mountains are God's also!

People: LET US WORSHIP THE CREATOR OF THE SEAS AND THE LANDS!

Collect

God of all wisdom, you are the source of all that is. Help us better to comprehend you: that, our limitations of human intellect overcome, we may stand in proper awe and wonder, humility and respect before you and the magnificent works of your divine mind. In Jesus' name we pray. Amen

Prayer of Confession

Eternal God, we confess our tendency to reduce you to our size and to lower you to our level by conceiving you in human terms and categories that cannot begin to comprehend your majesty and might, wisdom and wonder. Forgive us, we pray, and overcome both our natural limitations and our artificial restrictions, because of which we conceive you after our own image and likeness. Expand our minds at least enough for us to sense the utter mystery of your holiness, and for us to be moved to worship in wonder. In the name of Jesus we pray. Amen

Proper 16
Sunday between August 21 and August 27 inclusive

Gospel: Matthew 16:13-20

Theme: The testimony of the Church

Exegetical note: It should be surprising, if not sobering, to most congregations to find that in all of the Gospels, Jesus is quoted as using the word "church" only in Matthew, once here and twice in chapter 18. What we have, then, in Matthew's inflation of Mark's version of this incident is a retrospective testimony of the Church's recognition of Peter as its Rock, and of Jesus as God's "Son" as well as the Christ.

Call to Worship
(based on Psalm 95)

Leader: Come, let us worship and bow down!

People: LET US KNEEL BEFORE GOD, OUR MAKER!

Leader: For we are the people of God's pasture!

People: WE ARE THE SHEEP OF GOD'S HAND!

Collect

God of glory, you have placed upon your Church the responsibility of bearing witness to your will, word, and work. Make us worthy of this calling: that, assisted by your Spirit, our testimony may do justice to the good news you have given us in Christ Jesus. In his name we pray. Amen

Prayer of Confession

God of grace, we confess that as both individuals and your Church, we have failed miserably to bear the kind of witness that would do justice to your message of love, mercy, and forgiveness for the world. We have compounded the natural limitations of our human minds and tongues with our failure to take seriously our calling and task, and we have not served our gospel well. Forgive us, we pray, and help us to overcome every obstacle of heart, spirit, mind and body that keeps us from proclaiming your Christ and coming Reign. In Jesus' name we pray. Amen

Proper 17
Sunday between August 28 and September 3 inclusive

First Lesson: Exodus 19:1-9

Theme: Being borne on eagle's wings

Exegetical note: One of the most striking images of God in the Pentateuch appears in this passage: God is (like) an eagle, who bears the chosen people out of captivity and to God's very self. This underemployed image certainly "works" for both the people of the old covenant and those of the new as well.

Call to Worship
(based on Psalm 114)

Leader: Let the earth tremble before the presence of God!

People: LET THE MOUNTAINS QUAKE BEFORE THE GOD OF JACOB!

Leader: For God turns rocks into pools of water,

People: AND STONES INTO LIVING STREAMS!

Collect

Most high God, like a mother eagle you bore the children of Israel out of captivity and into freedom. Lift us likewise from the throes of sin: that, safe above that which holds us in bondage, we may be carried on your mighty wings to the heavenly blessings you have promised. In the name of Jesus we pray. Amen

Prayer of Confession

Most holy God, we confess that we sometimes grow comfortable in our captivity to sin, so that we neither seek nor even want the liberation that you can and will deliver; and we know that, as a result, we lead desperate and pointless lives. Forgive us, O God, and plant within us the seeds of discontent that will make us yearn for freedom and righteousness. Then rescue us from the evil bonds that have kept us from serving you and have numbed us to our wretchedness. In the name of the Christ we pray. Amen

Proper 17
Sunday between August 28 and September 3 inclusive

Second Lesson: Romans 12:1-13

Theme: The selves of the saved as sacrifices

Exegetical note: The first verse of this selection is a "hinge" or "pivot" between the soteriological explanations of chapters 1-11 and the ethical ones of 12-15. The connective word is "therefore," but the idea that really ties salvation to action is that the "bodies" (i.e., selves) of the saved are living sacrifices, which in turn are the proper worship of God (probably, for Paul, in addition to rather than as opposed to the cultic activity).

Call to Worship
(based on Psalm 114)

Leader: When Israel went forth from bondage in Egypt,

People: AND THE HOUSE OF JACOB WAS FREED FROM CAPTIVITY,

Leader: Israel became the realm of God's rule,

People: AND GOD'S PEOPLE BECAME GOD'S SANCTUARY!

Collect

Eternal God, you have called upon your people to be living sacrifices in the service of the gospel. Give us now the courage to meet that challenge: that, fortified by your Spirit, we may be able to face every hardship in the name of the Christ. In that name we meet and pray. Amen

Prayer of Confession

Everlasting God, we confess with great shame that we have been willing to give up little or nothing for the sake of the gospel, much less to sacrifice ourselves, as Saint Paul said we must. Forgive us our timidity and selfishness, we pray, and sow within us the seeds of commitment and courage that will cause us to dedicate ourselves whole-heartedly to ministry and mission in the service of the Christ and the coming Reign that you have promised. In Jesus' name we pray. Amen

Proper 17

Sunday between August 28 and September 3 inclusive

Gospel: Matthew 16:21-28

Theme: Judgment upon the Church

Exegetical note: Jesus' warnings here about the cost of discipleship — including cross-bearing and loss of life — culminate in the apocalyptic vision of the Son of Man coming in glory with angels to reward (or punish), not humanity in general, but the disciples, and precisely on the basis of their performance. This is a particularly Matthean warning to the Church of his own day.

Call to Worship

Leader: People of God, we are called to discipleship!

People: WE ARE CALLED TO SUFFERING AND SACRIFICE!

Leader: May we not be weighed and found wanting!

People: MAY WE NOT FAIL IN OUR WITNESS!

Collect

God of majesty, you have warned us of crosses to be borne in your service. Give us the courage to acknowledge and accept them: that, strengthened by your sustaining Spirit, we may be fearless in our proclamation of the gospel and constant in our faith in the Christ, in whose name we pray. Amen

Prayer of Confession

Merciful God, it embarrasses us to admit, to you and to ourselves, just how weak and timid we have been in our service to the gospel, and how reluctant to bear any hardship, much less a cross, in our Christian witness. Forgive us our faintheartedness, O God, and grant us a measure of your own infinite strength, so that we may be willing and able to face any terror and make any sacrifice in the fulfilling of our discipleship to Christ Jesus, in whose name we trust and pray. Amen

Proper 18
Sunday between September 4 and September 10 inclusive

First Lesson: Exodus 19:16-24

Theme: The awesome presence of God

Exegetical note: Every aspect of this narrative points to the awesomeness of the presence of God. The people's distant encounter with the Almighty is startling enough, affecting almost every sense; yet, they were kept at the foot of the mountain, protected from the direct experience of God that ostensibly they would not have been able to bear. Only Moses and Aaron are given the privilege of hearing God directly and (subsequently) mediating God's word and will.

Call to Worship
(based on Psalm 115)

Leader: Brothers and sisters, our God is in the heavens!

People: OUR GOD MADE THE HEAVENS AND THE EARTH!

Leader: Let all who fear God also trust in God!

People: FOR GOD IS OUR HELP AND OUR SHIELD!

Collect

God of infinite grandeur, you have given a few the privilege of a direct encounter with you. Let us see as much of you as we can bear: that, filled with the experience of you, we may better serve you in our age of doubt and disbelief. In Jesus' name we pray. Amen

Prayer of Confession

God of boundless grace, we confess that we often allow our lack of direct and dramatic experiences of you to lead us to doubt your very existence and to succumb to the skepticism of our modern age, and that we let the outlandish claims of self-proclaimed prophets compound our uncertainties. Forgive us, O God; convince us again that, precisely because you are Ultimate, your being and nature are unfathomable; and help us to trust in the testimony of those who have witnessed you directly, and in our own experiences in which you have touched us subtly. In the Christ's name we pray. Amen

Proper 18
Sunday between September 4 and September 10 inclusive

Second Lesson: Romans 13:1-10

Theme: The challenge of Christian citizenship

Exegetical note: The exhortation in the first seven verses of this selection would seem to mitigate against any sort of civil disobedience in the name of Christian conscience. But it must be read in the light of the fact that Christianity itself was an illegal sect (or "cult"!) in Paul's time (or soon after). It also must be balanced (as it has been throughout the history of Christian political ethics) by Acts 5:28 as a kind of "bottom line": "We must obey God rather than humans."

Call to Worship
(based on Psalm 115)

Leader: God has been mindful of us!

People: GOD WILL BLESS US!

Leader: God blessed the houses of Israel and Aaron!

People: GOD WILL BLESS ALL WHO FEAR GOD, BOTH THE GREAT AND THE SMALL!

Collect

Most just God, you have placed upon us the expectation of responsible citizenship in our earthly societies. Give us the wisdom to carry out this task: that, when demands of the state and claims of our faith seem to conflict, we may be guided to proper action by your Holy Spirit. In Jesus' name we pray. Amen

Prayer of Confession

God of all righteousness, we confess that we sometimes let our patriotism get out of hand, as well as our devotion to "law and order" and the status quo, and thus give the political powers that be an almost divine status. Forgive us, we pray, and help us to maintain the proper respect for those in secular authority, but to discern when in Christian conscience we must oppose them and their policies in the name of the sacred and the cause of the Christ. In his name we pray. Amen

Proper 18
Sunday between September 4 and September 10 inclusive

Gospel: Matthew 18:15-20

Theme: Handling conflict in a holy community

Exegetical note: The first few verses of this passage should serve as a reminder that, at least within the Christian fellowship, the inevitable conflicts that arise should be dealt with circumspectly. Rather than creating a *cause celebre* from the outset, a "wronged" party should attempt to resolve a grievance one-on-one with the perpetrator, and only then if not satistifed, and only gradually, attempt to seek resolution in a wider circle of consultation.

Call to Worship
(based on Psalm 114)

Leader: Brothers and sisters, the Church is a holy community!

People: THE CHURCH IS A GODLY FELLOWSHIP, NOT LIKE THE WORLD!

Leader: Let us therefore be to one another as a family!

People: LET US TREAT EACH OTHER AS CHILDREN OF THE MOST HIGH!

Collect

God of infinite power, you have cautioned your servants to be slow to anger. Teach us to resolve conflict in wholesome ways: that, touched by your love and understanding, we may deal with the inevitable disagreements that arise with fairness and grace. In the name of Jesus we pray. Amen

Prayer of Confession

God of exceeding patience, we confess that we do not always deal with differences of opinion in positive and productive ways, even within the Church, and that we sometimes vent our own personal frustrations in life by escalating petty issues to the level of grand causes, and make slight divergences of view into major disagreements that provoke hard feelings and arguments. Forgive us, O God, and help us to take to heart Saint Paul's advice to settle all matters in a Spirit of fellowship, harmony, and selfless love. In Jesus' name we pray. Amen

Proper 19
Sunday between September 11 and September 17 inclusive

First Lesson: Exodus 20:1-20

Theme: Other gods

Exegetical note: The commandments of the so-called "First Table," i.e., those dealing directly with God (vv. 2-4) actually reflect, not monotheism, but henotheism, i.e., the allegiance to one god without denying the existence of others, in this case the nature gods of the agricultural peoples with whom the Israelites came into contact. Far from reflecting a dated problem, however, the injunctions remind modern people of the many god-like concerns that claim ultimate allegiance.

Call to Worship
(based on Psalm 19)

Leader: The heavens declare God's glory!

People: THE FIRMAMENT PROCLAIMS GOD'S HANDIWORK!

Leader: If days and nights we poured forth words,

People: OUR TONGUES WOULD FAIL TO TELL OF GOD'S GRANDEUR!

Collect

Most holy One, you have told us to have no other gods before us. Place this commandment in our hearts: that, in the midst of all the things that demand our allegiance, we may devote ourselves only and completely to you. In the name of the Christ we pray. Amen

Prayer of Confession

God of Israel Old and New, we confess that we often allow ourselves to submit ourselves to the god-like claims and demands of modern life, and to allow them to compete with you as objects for our faith and devotion. Forgive us this idolatry, we pray, and remind us that the first of your commandments is that we have no other gods before us. Teach us to make you the axis of our lives, around which all other concerns and commitments revolve, and without which our lives turn into confusion and chaos. In the name of Jesus the Christ we pray. Amen

Proper 19
Sunday between September 11 and September 17 inclusive

Second Lesson: Romans 14:5-12

Theme: Christian tolerance

Exegetical note: Paul recognizes here, probably for the rectification of a problem of intolerance among the Roman Christians, that religious practices do not have to be uniform or universal. If Paul is to be taken at his word, then anything done or not done in good faith in the Christ is honorable, and works finally to the good of all.

Call to Worship
(based on Psalm 19)

Leader: May the words of our mouths be acceptable in God's sight!

People: MAY THE MEDITATIONS OF OUR HEARTS BE PLEASING TO GOD!

Leader: Let us strive to be blameless before God!

People: LET US YEARN TO BE INNOCENT AND FAULTLESS!

Collect

God of all people, you have taught us to be tolerant of one another, especially in matters of faith. Instill in us your Spirit of openness: that, seeing our religious expressions as relative, we may take only our faith in you and the Christ as absolute. In his name we pray. Amen

Prayer of Confession

God of all patience, we confess with great shame that we are not as tolerant of one another in religious matters as we should be, but create and perpetuate hostilities with one another over the rich variety of ways that people express their relationships to you. Forgive us such pettiness, O God, and encourage in us a deep appreciation for the depth of the human spirit and the richness of the human imagination. Convince us once and for all that there is no one right way to worship or serve you and that anything done in good faith in the Christ does honor to you, your Church, and your coming Reign. In Jesus' name we pray. Amen

Proper 19
Sunday between September 11 and September 17 inclusive

Gospel: Matthew 18:21-35

Theme: Limitless forgiveness

Exegetical note: The saying of Jesus about forgiveness and the loosely connected parable of the unforgiving, forgiven servant work together in this setting to suggest that forgiveness should be both limitless and contagious. Not only should one forgive without ceasing, but one who is forgiven should multiply the mercy by forgiving as well.

Call to Worship
(based on Psalm 19)

Leader: Let us bless the God of mercy!

People: LET US PRAISE THE GOD OF GRACE!

Leader: For to do wrong is human!

People: BUT TO FORGIVE IS THE WAY OF GOD!

Collect

God of absolute love, you have taught us in the words and life of Jesus to be forgiving without limit. Enable us to live according: that, our human passions turned into compassion, we may reflect the very grace that you have shown to us in Christ Jesus, in whose name we pray. Amen

Prayer of Confession

God of all compassion, we admit that we find forgiveness in any degree difficult, and unlimited pardon impossible because of our sin and the selfishness that it produces in us. Instead, we take offense easily, cultivate it carefully, and perpetuate it endlessly. Forgive us, we pray, and fill us with your Spirit of mercy and grace, which alone can help us to overcome the obstacles of heart, mind, and spirit that prevent us from exhibiting in even the most trivial situation the kind of forgiveness that Jesus showed to his torturers on Calvary. In his holy name we pray. Amen

Proper 20
Sunday between September 18 and September 24 inclusive

First Lesson: Exodus 32:1-14

Theme: Selfless intercession

Exegetical note: Modern readers will have difficulty with a view of God that allows for the divine wrath to get so out of hand that the deity has to be dissuaded from and repent of the vengeful evil that the divine indignation has threatened. More plausible, perhaps, is the selfless intercession of Moses, who gave up the flattering divine offer to become the new father of a great nation in order to plead on the basis of the old Abramic pact.

Call to Worship
(based on Psalm 106)

Leader: Sisters and brothers, let us never be as the Israelites in the wilderness!

People: FOR THEY REBELLED AGAINST THE MOST HIGH!

Leader: But let us remember God's steadfast love!

People: FOR IT SAVED EVEN THOSE WHOSE FAITH WAS WEAK!

Collect

Most generous God, you graciously answer the prayers of your people. Teach us to pray selflessly: that, placing the needs of others before our own, we shall let compassion rather than self-centeredness guide our intercessions to you. In the name of Jesus we pray. Amen

Prayer of Confession

All-compassionate God, we confess that we are selfish and self-centered in every area of our lives, but especially in our prayers. We ask you, not only for what we need, but for what we want, including the most trivial, and forget the dire situations caused by famine, natural disaster, disease, terrorism, war, and civil strife the world over. Forgive us, O God, and teach us not to pray for happiness while there is still hunger, possessions while there is still poverty, or peace of mind while there is still violence in the world. In the name of Christ Jesus we pray. Amen

Proper 20
Sunday between September 18 and September 24 inclusive

Second Lesson: Philippians 1:21-27

Theme: Continuity of life in Christ Jesus

Exegetical note: Paul, probably writing from prison, finds himself facing the real possibility of martyrdom, which he not only does not fear, but seems to welcome. His only hesitation stems from his suspicion that he may be more useful alive for those dependent on his guidance, and thus he resolves to continue "in the flesh." But in either case, alive or "departed," Paul is certain that he will continue to be "in Christ."

Call to Worship
(based on Psalm 106)

Leader: May God remember us and show us favor!

People: MAY GOD HELP US AND DELIVER US!

Leader: May God show us the prosperity of a chosen people!

People: MAY GOD PERMIT US TO GLORY IN OUR DIVINE HERITAGE!

Collect

Almighty God, you have created in Christ Jesus a community that transcends death. Instill in us a sense of oneness with all your saints: that, strengthened by that crowd of witnesses, we may become a timeless Church united against evil and for your gospel. In the name of the Christ we pray. Amen

Prayer of Confession

Ancient of days, it sorrows us deeply to confess how limited our sense of the community of the Christ is, and how much we identify "Church" with a building, congregation, or denomintaion, forgetting that it is a cosmic and universal body that transcends, not only our distinctions, but time and space as well. Forgive us, we pray; open our eyes, minds, and hearts to the extraordinary scope of the new Israel founded in Christ Jesus; and widen and deepen our commitment to being the people of your ageless will and eternal Word. In Jesus' name we pray. Amen

Proper 20
Sunday between September 18 and September 24 inclusive

Gospel: Matthew 20:1-16

Theme: God's gracious unfairness

Exegetical note: The original "punchline" to this parable was probably verse 15, which would shift the focus of the parable properly from the laborers to the vineyard owner and would underscore his generosity. The lesson, then, is about God and God's coming Reign: God will be just to all but "unfairly" gracious to some.

Call to Worship

Leader: Let us gather in the name of the God of glory!

People: LET US JOIN TO WORSHIP THE GOD OF GRACE!

Leader: For ours is a God of righteousness and justice!

People: OURS IS A GOD OF FORGIVENESS AND MERCY!

Collect

God of past, present, and future, you have promised a Reign that will bless humanity and the world. Set our sights upon this coming reality: that, inspired by the hope that it brings, we may know ourselves to be recipients of your incomparable grace and mercy. In Jesus' name we pray. Amen

Prayer of Confession

Merciful God, we confess that we have failed miserably to emulate your justice in our dealings with others, much less your graciousness, and that we have sown ill-will, contempt, hatred, and discord as a result. Forgive us, we pray, and inspire us by the mercy and forgiveness that you have shown to us in Christ Jesus to deal, not just honestly and fairly, but generously and charitably, after the example of Christ Jesus, who taught love for enemies and forgave even his tormentors. In his name and spirit we pray. Amen

Proper 21
Sunday between September 25 and October 1 inclusive

First Lesson: Exodus 33:12-23

Theme: God's unbearable majesty

Exegetical note: Face imagery permeates this selection. The preceding verse (11) has claimed that God spoke to Moses "face to face," and verse 14 has God promising that his "face" (presence) would go with Moses. But the following verses make it clear that no one, not even Moses, can look upon God's face and live. The majesty of God is simply more than mortals can take "head-on," so they must be content with viewing God's "backside" (v. 23).

Call to Worship
(based on Psalm 99)

Leader: God reigns! Let all people tremble!

People: GOD IS ENTHRONED! LET THE EARTH QUAKE!

Leader: God is great in Zion and exalted over all nations!

People: LET ALL PEOPLE PRAISE GOD'S GREAT AND TERRIBLE NAME!

Collect

Magnificent God, you have revealed of yourself as much as we need to know for our redemption. Spur our inquiring minds: that, questing after complete knowledge of you, we may gain an even better sense of your unfathomable being and unspeakable grandeur. In the name of the Christ we pray. Amen

Prayer of Confession

God of the universe, we confess that we sometimes grow frustrated at our inability to grasp more of your divine nature than we do, and that we sometimes even fall into skepticism about your existence, activity, and will. Forgive our impatience, O God, and continue to reveal yourself to us progressively, even as our understanding of the universe grows. If we cannot behold your face, then let us be satisfied with your handiwork, both in the cosmos and in the Christ. In his name we pray. Amen

Proper 21
Sunday between September 25 and October 1 inclusive

Second Lesson: Philippians 2:1-13

Theme: Christian selflessness

Exegetical note: It is understandable that the grandeur of the famous hymn here (vv. 5-11) might overshadow the exhortation that precedes it. But the two are intimately related. The self-emptying and self-humbling of Christ Jesus are to be the "mindset" of his followers: simply stated, they are to be as selfless toward one another as he was "unto death."

Call to Worship
(based on Psalm 99)

Leader: Holy is God: a mighty ruler and a lover of justice!

People: GOD HAS ESTABLISHED FAIRNESS AND RIGHTEOUSNESS!

Leader: Let us praise God's holy name!

People: LET US WORSHIP AT GOD'S FEET!

Collect

Eternal God, you have taught us through the words and life of Jesus to be selfless and humble. Lay this lesson upon our hearts afresh: that, emptied of our selves, we may be filled with his spirit of self-sacrifice and therein find our glory. In his name we pray. Amen

Prayer of Confession

Everliving God, it pains us to confess just how selfish, self-centered, and self-serving we really are, and thus how little like the Christ who gave his life for humanity. We try to know ourselves, find ourselves, better ourselves, and even remodel ourselves, all in an effort to overcome the effects of sin that only you can alleviate. Forgive us, we pray, and help us to follow the teachings and to emulate the life of Jesus, who emptied and humbled himself for us and thereby found glory in you. In his name and spirit we pray. Amen

Proper 21
Sunday between September 25 and October 1 inclusive

Gospel: Matthew 21:28-32

Theme: Religiousness that resists grace

Exegetical note: RSV and NEB give two very different versions of this passage, reversing, in effect, the sons' responses and, accordingly, changing the crowd's reply to Jesus' question. The point, however, remains the same: outcasts are far more ready to accept God's coming Reign than are the overtly religious, ostensibly because the latter's self-righteousness prevents them from responding to God's graciousness.

Call to Worship
(based on Psalm 99)

Leader: Let us praise our God!

People: LET US WORSHIP AT GOD'S HOLY MOUNTAIN!

Leader: For our God is holy!

People: OUR GOD IS HOLY INDEED!

Collect

God of heaven and earth, you are the author of our redemption. Save us now from our religious self-righteousness: that, forsaking all attempts to save ourselves by our worship or our works, we may at last place our faith only in your grace in Christ Jesus, in whose name we pray. Amen

Prayer of Confession

Compassionate God, we confess with dismay how much we place our faith in our religion rather than your righteousness, and in our own goodness rather than your grace; and we know in our hearts that, at best, we wind up self-righteous, and thus all the more insulated from your mercy and forgiveness. Forgive us, we pray, and remove us from the ranks of the Pharisees. Teach us our dependence upon your blessed actions in Christ Jesus, and help us to respond in thankfulness and praise for his wondrous work on our behalf. In his name we pray. Amen

Proper 22
Sunday between October 2 and October 8 inclusive

First Lesson: Numbers 27:12-23

Theme: Divine commission and human ordination

Exegetical note: In anticipation of his death, Moses asks God to select a successor for him, lest the Israelites be leaderless and therefore aimless. The "spirit" that God attributes to his appointee, Joshua, is ambiguous, but probably means an innate charisma, which nevertheless has to be supplemented by a measure of Moses' authority as well as the priest Eleazar's examination and (ostensibly) approval.

Call to Worship
(based on Psalm 81)

Leader: Sing aloud to God, our strength!

People: SHOUT FOR JOY TO JACOB'S GOD!

Leader: Raise a song! Sound the harp!

People: BLOW THE HORN! FOR THIS IS GOD'S DAY!

Collect

Eternal God, you have commissioned in every age individuals to carry on your work. Lay your hands upon us as well: that, as each generation of your servants rests from its labors, we may rise to take up the task of doing your work. In Jesus' name we pray. Amen

Prayer of Confession

Almighty God, we confess that we too often try to rely upon our own gifts when it comes to ministry and missions in your holy name, and seek neither your divine commission nor the ordination of our fellow Christians to strengthen us in our endeavors; and we know that our efforts in your service suffer as a result. Forgive us our prideful independence, O God, and teach us to seek always the power that comes from you and the strength in numbers that resides in your Church. In the name of the Christ we pray. Amen

Proper 22
Sunday between October 2 and October 8 inclusive

Second Lesson: Philippians 3:12-21

Theme: Perfection pursued, glory given

Exegetical note: Paul is apparently countering the contention of some among the Philippians who are claiming to have attained perfection and who, ironically, are living libertine lives as a result. Against them, Paul admits his own lack of, but hope for, perfection and his determination to press on toward it, knowing full well that his future glory lies not in his own effort, but the eschatological action of Christ Jesus.

Call to Worship
(based on Psalm 81)

Leader: May God lift our burdens!

People: MAY GOD LIGHTEN OUR LOADS!

Leader: May God answer us in the thunder!

People: MAY GOD TEST US AND FIND US WORTHY!

Collect

Most holy God, you have set before us in scripture the ideal of perfection. Propel us now toward that goal: that, whatever righteousness we are unable to achieve on our own, you will supplement with the action of your sustaining Spirit. In the name of Jesus we pray. Amen

Prayer of Confession

Forgiving God, it is unfortunately true that, since we do not expect to achieve perfection in this life, we quietly reject it as a goal, and aim for mere decency toward others as our best claim to holiness and godliness. Forgive us, O God, and remind us that whatever righteousness we are unable to attain through our own efforts will be graciously supplemented by you and your Holy Spirit, to the end that we shall be sanctified and glorified after the image and likeness of Christ Jesus. In his precious name we pray. Amen

Proper 22
Sunday between October 2 and October 8 inclusive

Gospel: Matthew 21:33-43

Theme: Claiming God's coming Reign

Exegetical note: Form-critical analysis of this passage in light of the other versions of the parable in the Synoptics and the Gospel of Thomas reveals that the original point of the story was not Christological; nor was it primarily allegorical. Rather, it was a simple, if shocking, "Kingdom" parable, whose point was the value of the coming Reign of God and the extraordinary, even desperate measures that the lowly should take in claiming it as their own.

Call to Worship

Leader: Brothers and sisters, let us renew our faith in God!

People: LET US GIVE OURSELVES TO GOD FROM THE DEPTHS OF OUR HEARTS!

Leader: Let us dedicate our very lives to God's coming Reign!

People: AND LET US VOW TO SACRIFICE ALL TO CLAIM IT AS OUR OWN!

Collect

Sovereign God, you have promised us your glorious Reign for the future. Help us now to claim it as our own: that, preparing for its coming glories, we may become participants in its present gifts, which abound even now in our imperfect world. In Jesus' name we pray. Amen

Prayer of Confession

Righteous God, we confess that we do not consistently keep your promised coming Reign before us as our goal, and that we settle all too eagerly for the world as it is, as if there were nothing else to look forward to; and we admit that such complacency and contentedness on our part denies your word and weakens our discipleship on behalf of you and your Christ. Forgive us, we pray, and inspire us anew with the parables of Jesus, which tell us of the glorious image of the wonderful future that you have in store for this suffering and sorrowful world. In his name we hope and pray. Amen

Proper 23
Sunday between October 9 and October 15 inclusive

First Lesson: Deuteronomy 34:1-12

Theme: The greatness of godliness

Exegetical note: The testimonial that concludes the poignantly moving account of Moses' death and secret burial (by none other than God!) within sight of the Promised Land suggests a timeless human truth: one's greatness should not be measured solely with reference to the accomplishment of grand goals, but with reference to the extent to which one has known and served God. For Moses fell short of his destination, but was nevertheless the most outstanding of Israel's prophets.

Call to Worship
(based on Psalm 135)

Leader: Praise God, you who stand in God's house!

People: LET US GIVE PRAISE IN THE COURTS OF GOD!

Leader: Praise God, for God is good!

People: SING TO GOD'S NAME, FOR GOD IS GRACIOUS!

Collect

Holy God, you have taught us by the example of your biblical heroes that greatness lies in godliness. Lay that lesson upon our hearts: that, abandoning all worldly standards of accomplishment and achievement, we may find true success in the doing of your will. In Jesus' name we pray. Amen

Prayer of Confession

Eternal God, we confess that our human values are all wrong, and that we admire as "successful" those who have achieved the fame, fortune, acclaim and admiration of this world, rather than those who have lived their lives for you, your Christ, and your coming Reign. Forgive us, we pray, and transform our hearts by the power of your Spirit, to the end that we shall hold in greatest esteem those who have lived most fully for you and those who have known and served you the best. In the name of Jesus the Christ we pray. Amen

Proper 23
Sunday between October 9 and October 15 inclusive

Second Lesson: Philippians 4:1-9

Theme: True peace of mind

Exegetical note: Paul obviously feels deep affection for the Philippian Christians, and his encouraging words here are heartfelt. His is much more than a cavalier "don't worry, be happy" admonition, however. His call for rejoicing and equanimity is firmly rooted in the expectation of Jesus' imminent return. That is the basis for the incomprehensible peace of mind — i.e., the peace of God! — that he promises them (twice!).

Call to Worship
(based on Psalm 135)

Leader: Sisters and brothers, rejoice! For our God is great!

People: OUR GOD IS ABOVE ALL GODS!

Leader: Let the house of Israel bless God!

People: LET ALL PEOPLE PRAISE GOD'S HOLY NAME!

Collect

God of righteousness, you have promised us perfect peace in Christ Jesus. Ease our troubled minds: that, our attention turned to future glories, our present worries about ourselves and our world will be dispelled and dissolved into hope. In the name of the Christ we pray. Amen

Prayer of Confession

Most merciful God, we confess that we are constantly beset by worries about ourselves, and particularly about our precarious places in an uncertain world. We are so preoccupied with the problems of the present, we are unable to pay attention to your promises of a bright and glorious Reign that awaits us in the future. Forgive us our short-sightedness, O God, and fill us again with hope. Refocus our eyes, hearts, minds, and spirits away from all that troubles us and upon the peace and joy that await us in the Christ. In his name we pray. Amen

Proper 23
Sunday between October 9 and October 15 inclusive

Gospel: Matthew 22:1-14

Theme: The "many called" of God

Exegetical note: Matthew has spliced together two originally independent parables (vv. 1-10 and 11-14) and allegorized them to speak to his contemporary situation. The original point of the first of these is that the coming Reign of God is to be populated by a motley assortment of outsiders — in this parable, "streetpeople" — rather than the respectable, invited, but finally unworthy ones (probably pious Jews) who had spurned the invitation. These are the "many called" of verse 14.

Call to Worship
(based on Psalm 135)

Leader: In heaven or on earth, whatever God pleases, God does!

People: GOD MAKES THE CLOUDS RISE AND THE RAINS FALL!

Leader: God sends lightning and winds!

People: LET US PRAISE THE GOD OF MIGHTY ACTS, WHO WILLS AND WORKS, SURPRISES AND SAVES!

Collect

Loving God, you have extended the invitation to participate in your coming Reign to all. Open our minds and hearts: that, freed of our prejudice against those we deem "unworthy," we may mirror your limitless love and boundless acceptance of humankind. In the name and spirit of Jesus we pray. Amen

Prayer of Confession

Mighty God, we are embarrassed to admit just how narrow-minded and biased we are against much of humanity because they do not live, act, speak, or see the world exactly as we do. Forgive us our pettiness, O God; free us from the smallness of spirit that grips us; empty us of our prejudice; and inspire us with the mind and ministry of Jesus, who extended your call to participate in your coming Reign even to the most despised and least religious of his day. In his holy name we pray. Amen

Proper 24
Sunday between October 16 and October 22 inclusive

First Lesson: Ruth 1:1-19a

Theme: A God for all

Exegetical note: The fact that the heroine of this story is not a Hebrew but a Moabite woman, and thus a traditional enemy of the Israelites suggests what, at the time of the writing, must have been an extraordinarily liberal idea, namely, that membership in God's chosen people should be open even to (hated) foreigners and that the God of Abraham could be their God, too. The fact that the book (named after this foreigner!) achieved canonical status suggests that the notion prevailed.

Call to Worship
(based on Psalm 146)

Leader: Let us praise God as long as we live!

People: LET US PRAISE GOD AS LONG AS WE BREATHE!

Leader: We shall not entrust ourselves to humankind!

People: WE SHALL RATHER FIND OUR HELP AND HOPE AND HAPPINESS IN GOD!

Collect

God of all humankind, your love and acceptance extends to all peoples. Make us as open as you: that, freed from the self-love that keeps us from affirming those unlike us, we may find ourselves more benevolent to all people everywhere. In the name of the Christ we pray. Amen

Prayer of Confession

Most compassionate God, we confess with shame that, while we affirm with our lips the worth of all people and their right to be called children of yours, in our hearts and minds we are full of prejudice and reservations, which keep us from accepting them as our brothers and sisters in Christ Jesus. Forgive us, we pray, and cleanse our spirits of the fears and biases that separate us from our neighbors as well as our enemies. Help us to feel a oneness with all humankind, as the family of God that we are. In Jesus' name we pray. Amen

Proper 24
Sunday between October 16 and October 22 inclusive

Second Lesson: 1 Thessalonians 1:1-10

Theme: Thoroughgoing monotheism

Exegetical note: Paul is apparently addressing here a number of people who had been polytheists or, more likely, henotheists — that is, devotees of one god ("idol" here) who nevertheless did not deny the reality of others. Thus he congratulates them on their having become monotheists, rejected the other gods as (mere) idols, and embraced the "living and true God." In Old Testament times even the Jews had been subject to henotheistic "lapses" into the worship of other gods (idols).

Call to Worship
(based on Psalm 146)

Leader: Happy are those whose help is the God of Jacob!

People: BLESSED ARE THOSE WHO WORSHIP THE ONE TRUE GOD!

Leader: For ours is the God who made heaven, earth, and all that is!

People: OURS IS THE GOD WHO KEEPS FAITH FOREVER!

Collect

God of being and action, you have revealed yourself as the one true God. Help us to resist the ongoing temptation to make and worship other divinities: that, freed from our idolatry, we may devote our hearts, minds, and spirits wholly to you. In Jesus' name we pray. Amen

Prayer of Confession

Most high God, we confess with deep sorrow our tendency to elevate minor concerns and attachments in our lives to divine status, and to devote ourselves to them as though they were gods. Forgive us this idolatry, O God; convince us by the power of your presence that you only are worthy of our affection and commitment; and help us at last to worship you alone in purity of heart as the very axis of our lives around which all else turns. In the name of Jesus the Christ we pray. Amen

Proper 24
Sunday between October 16 and October 22 inclusive

Gospel: Matthew 22:15-22

Theme: Separation of church and state

Exegetical note: The conversation depicted here must be understood in its original setting, in which the distinction between state and religion was blurred in a number of ways, not the least being the claim of the Roman emperor to be divine (and so designated on coins)! Jesus' famous dictum about "rendering," therefore, is a cleverly "safe" way of dealing with a question meant to entrap him, but also a profound statement about the appropriate separation between the secular and the sacred provinces, and thus between state and church.

Call to Worship

Leader: Sisters and brothers, let us render unto God that which is due!

People: LET US GIVE GOD GLORY AND HONOR!

Leader: Let us give God thanks and praise!

People: LET US GIVE GOD OUR FAITH AND HOPE, NOW AND FOREVER!

Collect

Living God, you have given us in scripture guidelines for weighing our many allegiances. Give us now the wisdom to choose well: that, beset by conflicting claims, we may know how best to serve you. In the name of the Christ we pray. Amen

Prayer of Confession

Merciful God, we admit with great shame how, in the midst of conflicting claims and commitments, we often lose sight of our responsibilities to you, your Christ, and your coming Reign. We let the demands of family, friendship, business, and even country take precedence over our duties on your behalf, and wind up being, at best, half-hearted Christians and part-time disciples. Forgive us, we pray, and assist us in reordering our priorities, so that our ministry in Jesus' name will come first and permeate everything else that we do. In that name we pray. Amen

Proper 25
Sunday between October 23 and October 29 inclusive

First Lesson: Ruth 2:1-13

Theme: Grace begets grace

Exegetical note: It is not entirely clear whether Ruth set out for or happened onto Boaz' field, since the wording of the first three verses suggests both. In any case, it is certain that Boaz' motive for being especially gracious to Ruth is that she had been likewise gracious to her mother in-law (and his kinswoman), Naomi. The moral of this story would seem to be that, at least in some situations, grace begets grace.

Call to Worship
(based on Psalm 128)

Leader: Blessed are those who fear God!

People: BLESSED ARE THOSE WHO WALK IN GOD'S WAYS!

Leader: May all God's people live in peace!

People: MAY ALL GOD'S PEOPLE PROSPER!

Collect

Most loving God, you have given us the grace we need to make us whole. Let that grace beget grace in us: that, realizing the love and mercy you have shown to us, we may now extend it to others. In the name of Christ Jesus we pray. Amen

Prayer of Confession

Most compassionate God, it saddens us to admit to ourselves, much less to you, how eagerly we have accepted the grace, mercy, and forgiveness that you have extended to us, but how slowly, reluctantly, and rarely we have been willing to do unto others as you have done to us. Forgive us, we pray, and teach and coax us to return grace for grace, mercy for mercy, and forgiveness for forgiveness, and thus to become the godly and righteous people that in Christ you have made it possible for us to be. In his precious name we pray. Amen

Proper 25
Sunday between October 23 and October 29 inclusive

Second Lesson: 1 Thessalonians 2:1-8

Theme: Proclaiming to please God

Exegetical note: Someone has apparently questioned Paul's motives in preaching the gospel, for he is moved here to deny the "charges" of error, immorality, deception, flattery, greed, and self-aggrandizement. His defense is pure and simple: his only motivation in preaching has been to please God, not other people.

Call to Worship

Leader: Let us proclaim the mighty works of God!

People: LET US TELL OF GOD'S POWER AND MIGHT!

Leader: Let us declare God's goodness and grace!

People: LET US AFFIRM GOD'S MERCY AND LOVING KINDNESS!

Collect

Almighty God, you have given us a Christ to trust and a gospel to proclaim. Help us to keep our motives pure: that, our personal objectives set aside, all that we say and do in your name may be to your glory and the proclamation of your coming Reign. In Jesus' name we pray. Amen

Prayer of Confession

Most merciful God, we are ashamed to confess just how often we deal with our fellow human beings out of selfish motives and for self-serving purposes, and how hypocritically we act as though we were generous and giving, when in fact we are seeking our own ends. Forgive us our lack of integrity, we pray, and establish in our hearts the vocation that we have to care for others in your name. Make us authentic agents of your gospel, sacrificial servants of your coming Reign, and dedicated disciples of your Christ, in whose name we pray. Amen

Proper 25
Sunday between October 23 and October 29 inclusive

Gospel: Matthew 22:34-46

Theme: Christian love as bifocal

Exegetical note: In a sense, Jesus refuses here to play along with the Pharisee's question, which called for a singular answer. Jesus' answer, advocating a "bifocal" love, was not original in the rabbinic tradition. Others had emphasized these two Old Testament injunctions before. Jesus does, however, appear to raise the second commandment to a nearly co-equal status with the first with the word "like" in v. 39, and in his citing both as the foundation for the law and the prophets.

Call to Worship

Leader: Let us love God with our hearts and souls!

People: LET US LOVE GOD WITH OUR MINDS AND STRENGTH!

Leader: Let us love our neighbors as ourselves!

People: FOR THIS IS THE WILL OF GOD AND THE GREATEST OF GOD'S COMMANDMENTS!

Collect

Most holy God, you have commended to us a love for you as well as for our fellow humans. Now implant that twofold affection within us: that, thus in tune with the sprit of your law, we may live so as to fulfill all of its precepts in righteousness and holiness. In Jesus' name we pray. Amen

Prayer of Confession

God of the ages, we confess that we are far better at talking about love and declaring love than at actualizing love and living love; and that much of the love we profess for you never quite finds expression in our attitudes and actions towards our fellow human beings. Forgive us, we pray, and convince us that the two kinds of love taught by Jesus were not independent options from which we may choose, but equally binding and mutually reinforcing expectations for which we are responsible as disciples of the Christ. In his name we pray. Amen

Proper 26
Sunday between October 30 and November 5 inclusive

First Lesson: Ruth 4:7-17

Theme: Small human events in God's great plan

Exegetical note: The key idea in this selection is that people behaving righteously in small events of everyday human concerns can become unwitting but crucial agents in God's unfolding salvation history. Ruth's earlier faithfulness to Naomi in adopting God and Israel as her own, and Boaz' graciousness toward Naomi in providing her a next of kin, work together to establish the line of none other than Israel's greatest king, David.

Call to Worship
(based on Psalm 127)

Leader: Unless God builds the house, the workers labor in vain!

People: UNLESS GOD WATCHES OVER THE CITY, THE GUARDS PROTECT IT FOR NOUGHT!

Leader: May our daily actions be for God's glory!

People: MAY OUR HUMAN CONCERNS WORK FOR SALVATION!

Collect

Good and true God, you have given us many examples in scripture of small human acts that were important parts of your divine plan. Guide us in the little things of everyday life: that, with your divine help, even the seemingly insignificant good that we accomplish may further your work on earth. In Jesus' name we pray. Amen

Prayer of Confession

Merciful God, we admit that much of what we do results from our desire to "play to the crowds" and to win acclaim, and that we therefore undervalue the important role that everyday righteousness can play in your divine plan. Forgive us our delusions of grandeur, O God, and narrow our focus to the smaller scale of daily life. Take our little successes and accomplishments in living your gospel, and make them work for the glory of your coming Reign and the Christ who proclaimed it. In his holy name we pray. Amen

Proper 26
Sunday between October 30 and November 5 inclusive

Second Lesson: 1 Thessalonians 2:9-13, 17-20

Theme: God's word at work

Exegetical note: Verse 13 here depicts Paul's paradoxical view that God's word has worked dynamically in himself in such a way that his words to them have actually amounted to the very word of God. Since he states that the same word is at work in all believers, his implication is that their own words may convey God's word as well.

Call to Worship

Leader: Sisters and brothers, we are gathered to proclaim the word of God!

People: WE MEET TO HEAR THE WORD OF GOD!

Leader: The word of God is at work within us!

People: THE WORD OF GOD IS FLOWING THROUGH US!

Collect

Eternal God, you have implanted your Word, not just in your greatest saints, but in all believers as well. Activate it within us: that, energized by its redemptive power, we may perform works to the benefit of others and the glory of you. In the name of Christ Jesus we pray. Amen

Prayer of Confession

God of wondrous love, we confess with shame that we have not tapped the power of your holy Word that you most graciously have instilled in us; that we have relied too much on our own abilities and strengths; and that we have failed to do justice to your holy gospel as a result. Forgive us, we pray, and give us the wisdom to search within ourselves for your divine power, the good fortune to find it, and the good sense to use it in our efforts to convey your saving word. In the name of the Christ we pray. Amen

Proper 26
Sunday between October 30 and November 5 inclusive

Gospel: Matthew 23:1-12

Theme: Hypocrisy vs. humility

Exegetical note: The words of Jesus related by Matthew here against the behavior of the scribes and Pharisees are timeless, for the hypocrisies that are catalogued reflect a spiritual arrogance and pride that place the authors of the pronouncements "above it all," an attitude symbolized by their love for regalia and titles. It is no accident, therefore, that the passage ends with a commendation of humility.

Call to Worship

Leader: People of God, let us worship the Most High!

People: LET US PRAISE THE AUTHOR OF ALL CREATION!

Leader: Let us lift our hearts and voices in adoration!

People: MAY OUR THOUGHTS AND WORDS RESOUND TO THE GLORY OF GOD!

Collect

Great God, you have warned us against the sin of hypocrisy and the pride that spawns it. Sow humility in our hearts: that, knowing our proper place relative to your majesty, we may be effective agents of your will and compassionate sisters and brothers of our neighbors. In Jesus' name we pray. Amen

Prayer of Confession

Everloving God, we acknowledge with great sorrow our tendency to enjoy the limelight and the attention that even our work in service of the gospel draws to us; and we admit with shame how much we relish the attention that comes our way, even from our most casual service to the Christ. Forgive us our pride and conceit, O God, and inspire us with the humility exhibited and commanded by Jesus, who, though his origin and destiny were in glory, found godliness in the lowliest of places and people. In his name we pray. Amen

Proper 27
Sunday between November 6 and November 12 inclusive

First Lesson: Amos 5:18-24

Theme: End-time expectations

Exegetical note: The warning of Amos is against the presumption of those among his own people who were looking forward to "the day of the Lord" — i.e., Jahweh's ultimate eschatological act on their behalf — with great anticipation. His suggestion is that those who want it most to come are those who understand it least, for it will be an event of darkness and gloom (i.e., catastrophe) for *everyone.*

Call to Worship
(based on Psalm 50)

Leader: Let us offer God a sacrifice of thanksgiving!

People: LET US PAY OUR VOWS TO THE MOST HIGH!

Leader: Let us call upon God in the day of trouble!

People: FOR GOD WILL DELIVER US, AND WE SHALL GLORIFY GOD!

Collect

God of redemption, you have instilled in us a hope for your final consummation of history. Keep us now from idle speculation: that, trusting you to act in good time, we may make every moment count in your service and to your glory. In Jesus' holy name we pray. Amen

Prayer of Confession

God of reconciliation, we confess that we are guilty of using the expectation of your end-time victory over evil as an excuse to neglect our present-day responsibility to minister to the world's need in your name. We spend more time wondering about when the Christ will come again than being the body of the Christ now. Forgive us, we pray, and make our expectation of your glorious Reign an inspiration for us to manifest its mercies in the here-and-now. In the name of the coming Christ we pray. Amen

Proper 27
Sunday between November 6 and November 12 inclusive

Second Lesson: 1 Thessalonians 4:13-18

Theme: Unity with Christ Jesus

Exegetical note: Despite Paul's earlier assurances of the imminence of Jesus' *parousia,* some of the faithful Thessalonians have died waiting for it, and their loved ones are grieving that the departed will not participate in the anticipated event. His hope and his imagery sound dated today, but not his assurance in verse 18 of the ongoing "togetherness" of the Christian believer with the Christ.

Call to Worship
(based on Psalm 50)

Leader: From the rising to the setting of the sun, God shines forth!

People: GOD SPEAKS AND SUMMONS THE WORLD!

Leader: Our God does not come quietly, but in tempest and fire!

People: GOD CALLS TO THE HEAVENS, AND THEY DECLARE GOD'S RIGHTEOUSNESS!

Collect

Almighty God, you have given us a tremendous source of hope in the promise of the second coming of your Christ. Make us now aware of our ongoing oneness with him: that, realizing our present unity with him, we may be active in our continuing mission until he comes. In his precious name we pray. Amen

Prayer of Confession

Faithful God, we confess that, when we look at our troubled world, we often despair at our ability to do anything at all to help it, and sometimes use the conviction that Jesus will come again and fix it all as an excuse to sit back and do nothing except long for that day. Forgive us, we pray, and make our faith in the coming of the Christ a stimulus rather than a sedative: let it inspire us and instill in us a righteous resolve to spread your love, justice, and peace until Jesus comes. In his name we pray. Amen

Proper 27
Sunday between November 6 and November 12 inclusive

Gospel: Matthew 25:1-13

Theme: Parousia and preparedness

Exegetical note: On the lips of Jesus this parable was probably about the coming Reign of God and the urgency of preparedness. But for Matthew it is about the delay of the *parousia* experienced by the Church of his own day (some half-century later), which by the twentieth century looks more like a non-occurrence. The challenge today, then, is to interpret meaningfully how the Christ comes "again" in our own time and what Christian watchfulness might mean now.

Call to Worship

Leader: Sisters and brothers, we are called to be prepared!

People: WE ARE CALLED TO BE READY FOR THE COMING OF THE CHRIST!

Leader: For the work of God is not yet finished!

People: THE REIGN OF GOD IS NOT YET ESTABLISHED!

Collect

Holy God, your scriptures give us hope for the coming of both your Reign and the Christ. Guide us now in the meantime: that, inspired by these future prospects, we may remain prepared for their arrival and preoccupied with our task to realize their glories in our own ministries. In Jesus' name we pray. Amen

Prayer of Confession

Heavenly God, we confess that we often let the prospects of the dawn of your Reign and of the arrival of the Christ fade from our minds, and that we therefore do not use them as images to inspire us or goals to guide us in our ongoing discipleship in the name of Jesus. Forgive us, we pray, and keep us constantly prepared, not just for the Reign that is to come but for the Reign that is already in our midst, and not just for the ultimate Second Coming, but for all of the many present comings of the Christ, especially in the least of our brothers and sisters. In his name we pray. Amen

Proper 28
Sunday between November 13 and November 19 inclusive

First Lesson: Zephaniah 1:7, 12-18

Theme: The jealousy of God

Exegetical note: Writing in the days of the reformer King Josiah and the prophet Jeremiah, Zephaniah was preoccupied with the impending doom that he foresaw in the coming "day of the Lord," which for him would be an event of divine wrath and human anguish. The omitted verses of this chapter indicate that what "set God off" so was that his chosen people had fallen into the worship of such foreign deities as Baal and Milcom, so that the foretold catastrophes were evidence of God's jealousy.

Call to Worship
(based on Psalm 76)

Leader: Glorious is God, more majestic than the eternal mountains!

People: AND TERRIBLE IS GOD, BEFORE WHOSE ANGER NO ONE CAN STAND!

Leader: For God utters judgments from the heavens!

People: GOD JUDGES TO SAVE THE WORLD'S OPPRESSED!

Collect

Most glorious God, you have warned us through scriptures about the dangers of idolatry. Keep us from the worship of false gods: that, concentrating only on you, we may be faithful to our calling as disciples of the Christ. In his name only do we pray. Amen

Prayer of Confession

Most gracious God, we are sorry to admit how much and how often we are tempted to take various commitments that we have in our lives too seriously, to set them up as other gods besides you, and to give them priority over our worship and work in your holy name. Forgive us, O God, and strengthen our loyalty and faith with your Holy Spirit. Make us single-minded in our devotion to you and true-hearted in our discipleship to Christ Jesus, in whose holy name we trust and pray. Amen

Proper 28
Sunday between November 13 and November 19 inclusive

Second Lesson: 1 Thessalonians 5:1-11

Theme: Moral support among Christians

Exegetical note: Paul's earlier utterances to the Thessalonians apparently had led them to believe that the *parousia* of the Christ was very near at hand, and to engage in speculation about "the times and the seasons." In response, Paul reminds them of the words of Jesus about that day coming "like a thief in the night," an image that he uses to contrast them as "day people," who should remain wakeful and sober, and who should — instead of engaging in idle speculation — give each other moral support.

Call to Worship

Leader: Let the household of faith be glad!

People: LET THE PEOPLE OF GOD REJOICE!

Leader: For God's coming Reign is at hand!

People: GOD'S SAVING RULE IS IN OUR MIDST!

Collect

God of promise and fulfillment, you have given us one another as fellow believers and disciples of the Christ. Help us to be truly supportive of each other: that, until your Reign comes in all its glory, we may live and work as a Church united by the hope we share. In Jesus' name we pray. Amen

Prayer of Confession

God of all ages, we confess that, as a Church, we are not always as supportive of one another as we should be and as you would like us to be. We use disagreements over belief and practices, and even budgets and personalities to foster disunity, and thus to get in the way of our being a loving community in ministry for you. Forgive us, we pray, and help us to put aside petty differences, so that we can at last live as your holy family and as effective disciples of your gospel in Christ Jesus. In his name we pray. Amen

Proper 28
Sunday between November 13 and November 19 inclusive

Gospel: Matthew 25:14-30

Theme: Preserving vs. promoting the gospel

Exegetical note: Exactly what Jesus' original intent was for this parable is uncertain, but the fearful, "protectionist" mentality of the third servant is universal and timeless: he timidly decides to protect what he has rather than to develop it, and because of his subsequent actions he is pronounced "wicked and lazy." This story could be applied to a myriad of cases, but its most likely referrent here is to those who would be preservers of the Gospel rather than promoters of it.

Call to Worship

Leader: Let the children of God sing praises!

People: LET THE FAMILY OF GOD GIVE THANKS!

Leader: Let the household of faith be glad for what God has given!

People: LET US ALL BE GOOD AND FAITHFUL SERVANTS OF THE MOST HIGH!

Collect

Creator God, you have given us a most gracious gift in the gospel. Help us to use wisely that precious treasure: that, keeping it not to ourselves, we may promote it effectively to the service of you and the salvation of the world. In the name and selfless spirit of Christ Jesus we pray. Amen

Prayer of Confession

Caring God, we confess with the deepest shame that we too often keep the good news that you have given us in the Christ to ourselves, as though we were to preserve rather than to proclaim it. We worry about creeds and confessions, principles and policies, and meanwhile forget that our first task is to carry your good news to the world. Forgive us, we pray, and commission us again with our apostolic charge. Make us yearn and burn to share the message of your grace in Christ Jesus with all people everywhere. In his holy name we pray. Amen

Proper 29
*Sunday between November 20 and November 26 inclusive
(Christ the King)*

First Lesson: Ezekiel 34:11-16, 20-24

Theme: God's fat and lean sheep

Exegetical note: Speaking as God's voice, Ezekiel lambasts the kings ("shepherds") of Isarel whose poor leadership led to their defeat and exile (vv. 1-10). God then vows to take over as their "shepherd," to restore and protect them, and to set up David (or "a" David) in that position. But the sheep themselves will have to undergo judgment, to separate the "fat" (i.e., those Israelites who have prospered at the expense of their own people while in exile) from the "lean" (i.e., their victims).

Call to Worship
(based on Psalm 23)

Leader: With God as our shepherd, we shall not want!

People: GOD PROVIDES RESTING PLACES FOR OUR BODIES!

Leader: God gives us refreshment for our souls!

People: GOD GIVES US RIGHTEOUS PATHS TO FOLLOW! THANKS BE TO GOD!

Collect

Eternal God, you have promised eventual judgment upon those inside and outside your fold. Make us and keep us righteous: that, whenever the time comes for your discernment, we shall be worthy to stand with your saints as faithful servants of you and Christ Jesus. In his name we pray. Amen

Prayer of Confession

Everloving God, we confess that we who bear the name of the Christ often treat one another unfairly and deal with each another unjustly, rather than as members of your holy family and brothers and sisters of Jesus. Forgive us, we pray, and implant your Spirit of love and righteousness in us. Make us to function less like a business or a club and more like your Church, the Body of the Christ, whose members work for the good of one another and the life of the whole. In the name of Jesus we pray. Amen

Proper 29
Sunday between November 20 and November 26 inclusive
(Christ the King)

Second Lesson: 1 Corinthians 15:20-28

Theme: God's ultimate intimacy

Exegetical note: The "kingship" that Paul projects here for the Christ (vv. 24ff.) is for a limited time (see "until" in v. 25), during which a war is to be waged with evil. Thereafter, the Christ ("Son" here) will be subjected to God, so that God may become "all in all." This final image, like all eschatological (and especially apocalyptic) thought, is open to a wide variety of interpretation, but at least signals a heretofore unknown intimacy between the Creator and Creation.

Call to Worship
(based on Psalm 23)

Leader: God is our protector from the shadow of death!

People: GOD IS OUR GUARDIAN FROM THE THROES OF EVIL!

Leader: God gives us comfort and sustenance!

People: GOD GIVES US GOODNESS AND MERCY FOREVER!

Collect

God of Creation, you have promised a day when you would be all in all. Give us a taste of that divine intimacy now: that, feeling you within ourselves and all creatures, we may experience a new oneness with you and your universe. In the cosmic name of the Christ we pray. Amen

Prayer of Confession

God of compassion, we confess that we let the genuine Otherness of your transcendent nature become an excuse for treating you as remote and removed from our everyday world, and aloof and alien to our daily lives. We numb ourselves to your presence, mistake your silence for absence, and fail completely to sense our deep and abiding spiritual unity with you. Forgive us, we pray, and touch us again with your Holy Spirit. Make us feel truly one with you, with Christ Jesus, and with all who share your wondrous creation with us. In Jesus' name we pray. Amen

Proper 29
Sunday between November 20 and November 26 inclusive
(Christ the King)

Gospel: Matthew 25:31-46

Theme: Royal approval for righteous action

Exegetical note: Whether "the least" of the "brethren" (vv. 40, 45) meant specifically the disciples who were to be received as envoys of Jesus or more generally the outcast and oppressed for whom Jesus consistently showed concern is a matter of dispute. In either case, however, it is clear that those who wind up on the eschatological "King's" right hand (or "good side," in today's parlance) and inherit the "Kingdom" are those who not only are righteous, but act righteously (i.e., compassionately) towards those in need.

Call to Worship

Leader: Let the world rejoice and its people be glad!

People: FOR THE REIGN OF GOD IS AT HAND!

Leader: Let the heavens shout and the earth jump for joy!

People: FOR CHRIST JESUS REIGNS, NOW AND FOREVER!

Collect

Most holy God, you have taught us not only to be righteous but also to act righteously, especially toward those in need. Touch us with your grace: that, seeing the Christ even in the least of our own, we may extend our love and compassion. In Jesus' holy name we pray. Amen

Prayer of Confession

God our Help in every age, we confess that we have failed miserably to seek out the image of the Christ in the least of our brothers and sisters, and have even figured out ways to feel righteous with respect to them, even while we were avoiding our responsibilities toward them. Forgive us, O God, and implant compassion in our hearts. Set before us again the ministry and message of Jesus, which sought out the outcast and oppressed, and treated them as important members of your holy family. In his name we pray. Amen

All Saints' Day
(or First Sunday in November)

First Lesson: Revelation 7:9-17

Theme: The saints' ultimate reward

Exegetical note: The powerful scene here is best appreciated against the backdrop of the reign of Emperor Domitian, toward the end of which (c. A.D. 96) John of Patmos was writing. Domitian was second only to Nero in his harshness toward Christians, and the "multitude" of saints pictured here, therefore, are those martyred under him and now vindicated and positioned before God's throne to serve as well as to be given the ultimate reward: shelter, solace, and shepherding by (in an ironic twist) a Lamb!

Call to Worship

Leader: Rejoice, Christians, for salvation belongs to our God!

People: REJOICE, INDEED, FOR REDEMPTION IS IN GOD'S LAMB!

Leader: Blessing and glory and thanksgiving to our God!

People: HONOR AND POWER AND MIGHT TO OUR GOD FOREVER AND EVER!

Collect

Wondrous God, you have promised ultimate vindication for all your saints. Keep us faithful to your will: that, despite the trials and temptations that we encounter, we may meet your coming Reign as more than conquerors by your grace in Christ Jesus, in whose name we pray. Amen

Prayer of Confession

God of all mercy, we confess that it takes very few and very small trials or temptations to distract us from our calling to ministry on your behalf and in the name of Jesus. In fact, we use every possible excuse and rationalization to avoid doing your work and being the disciples that we ought to be. Forgive us, we pray, and fortify our faith by the power of your Holy Spirit. Make us at last the servants of your coming Reign and the living Christ that we can and shall be with your help. In Jesus' name we pray. Amen

All Saints' Day
(or First Sunday in November)

Second Lesson: 1 John 3:1-3

Theme: God's unfinished children

Exegetical note: The writer here is probably countering the Gnostic belief that was circulating in the early church that saving knowledge (*gnosis*) brought instant perfection. Verse 2 here makes it clear that, while Christians are indeed God's children now, they are in a sense "unfinished," for their ultimate destiny is to be like Christ Jesus at the *parousia*. Meanwhile, says the following verse, hope purifies the believer.

Call to Worship
(based on Psalm 34)

Leader: Let us bless God at all times!

People: LET GOD'S PRAISE BE CONTINUALLY ON OUR LIPS!

Leader: Let our souls boast in God!

People: LET THE AFFLICTED HEAR AND BE GLAD!

Collect

Almighty God, you have graciously adopted us into your family despite our many faults. Make us to see ourselves as "unfinished" children of yours: that, convinced of our imperfections, we may grow in your grace into the likeness of the perfect Christ. In his name we pray. Amen

Prayer of Confession

All-loving God, we confess our almost irresistible tendency to be self-righteous and, because we are Christians, to consider ourselves better than most others and perfect in comparison to some. Forgive us our conceit, O God, and force us to take a long, hard look at ourselves and to see just how unfinished and imperfect we are. Move us beyond the salvation that we have by your merciful grace, and guide us through the process of sanctification, by which, with the help of your Spirit, we shall grow into true children of yours in the image of the Christ. In his name we pray. Amen

All Saints' Day
(or First Sunday in November)

Gospel: Matthew 5:1-12

Theme: The features and the future of saints

Exegetical note: Matthew's version of the Beatitudes is a bit more interpretive of Jesus' actual teachings than Luke's version. For this particular Sunday, the sayings are best taken as revealing the features of true saints: they are poor in spirit, gentle, "hungry" for justice, merciful, pure-hearted, peace-making, reviled and persecuted, and (probably because of these last two) sorrowful. But, as the second clause of each beatitude shows, they also have a promising future.

Call to Worship
(based on Psalm 34)

Leader: Let us magnify God and exalt God's name!

People: LET US LOOK TO GOD AND BE RADIANT!

Leader: Taste and see that God is good!

People: HAPPY ARE THE SAINTS WHO TAKE REFUGE IN GOD!

Collect

Glorious God, by your grace you have made us a people of faith with a promising future. Fix our gazes on your coming Reign: that, inspired by the vision of that wonderful prospect, we may grow in all of the traits that befit your saints. In the name of Christ Jesus we pray. Amen

Prayer of Confession

Gracious God, we confess that we do not desire or emulate sainthood as we should, and that we do not invest ourselves in the sanctification process that, by your grace and the help of your Spirit, would increase us in holiness and lead us toward the perfect image of the Christ. Forgive us, we pray, and let us not be so contented and complacent. Stir our souls and stimulate our spirits, so that we shall be restless and dissatisfied until we exhibit all of the marks and gifts of sainthood described in your Word. In the inspiring name of Jesus we pray. Amen

Thanksgiving Day

First Lesson: 1 Kings 8:55-61

Theme: Reestablishing the covenant

Exegetical note: This selection is from the closing benediction of Solomon's prayer at the dedication of his temple. In it he prays, on the one hand, that God continue to be present and to enable the people to keep the covenant, and, on the other hand, that the people be completely faithful to God. The passage reminds us that days of national celebration and thanksgiving are great opportunities to reestablish a people's covenant with God.

Call to Worship
(based on Psalm 138)

Leader: Let us give thanks to God with all our hearts!

People: LET US SING GOD'S PRAISES FOR ALL TO HEAR!

Leader: Let us give gratitude for God's steadfast love and faithfulness!

People: LET US EXALT GOD'S NAME AND WORD!

Collect

Most generous God, you have provided us so much for which to be thankful. Let us now use this day of thanksgiving as an opportunity for renewal: that, our covenant with you reestablished, we may become your people as never before, determined to multiply your mercies and gifts for all humankind. In Jesus' name we pray. Amen

Prayer of Confession

God of all blessings, we confess with tremendous shame that we have used our Thanksgiving celebrations as opportunities to be self-satisfied and self-congratulating, rather than as occasions to rededicate ourselves to you and our work on behalf of those who do not enjoy our advantages. Forgive us, we pray, and encourage us to live as your children of light in a world of darkness, and as your agents of grace among people who are hopeless now, but who by your grace may yet have reason to give thanks. In the name of Christ Jesus we pray. Amen

Thanksgiving Day

Second Lesson: 1 Corinthians 1:3-9

Theme: Gifts that tide Christians over

Exegetical note: In this opening to his epistle, Paul gives thanks for the spiritual gifts that the Corinthians have been given, and even singles out the very two (speech and knowledge) about which he will later express misgivings, at least with respect to their application among these people. The reference to the *parousia*, however, makes it clear that these are gifts to "tide them over" until "the end."

Call to Worship
(based on Psalm 145)

Leader: Great is God and greatly to be praised!

People: THE GREATNESS OF GOD IS UNSEARCHABLE!

Leader: Let us meditate on God's magnificent majesty and wondrous works!

People: LET US PRAISE GOD'S MIGHTY ACTS FROM GENERATION TO GENERATION!

Collect

Most giving God, you have provided well for human needs in every generation. Make us to see the blessings we have now as provisional: that, sensing the greater things that your coming Reign has in store, we may shed our contentedness and strive the harder to spread your word and do your work until the Christ comes. In his name we pray. Amen

Prayer of Confession

Blessed God, we confess with enormous shame that, when we think of those things for which we should be thankful, it is not your spiritual gifts that prefigure your coming Reign that come to mind, but the material possessions that merely dress our everyday lives. Forgive us our short-sightedness, O God, and help us to use this Thanksgiving Day as an opportunity to reflect upon the benefits from you that really matter, and to respond in thanks to you for the many blessings that you have provided for our souls until your Reign comes in all its glory. In the name of Jesus we pray. Amen

Thanksgiving Day

Gospel: Matthew 6:25-33

Theme: God's providence and priorities

Exegetical note: This passage probably was not originally a part of the Sermon on the Mount, since Luke locates it elsewhere. The exhortation against anxiety here has two bases, the first of which is the more developed: (1) God's providence and (2) God's priorities, namely, God's Reign and righteousness. The assurance throughout is that because of these things, everything else will "fall into place."

Call to Worship
(based on Psalm 65)

Leader: Give thanks to the God who nourishes the earth!

People: GIVE THANKS TO THE GOD WHO WATERS IT!

Leader: The pastures and hills drip with joy!

People: THE MEADOWS AND VALLEYS SHOUT AND SING!

Collect

Great provider God, you have given us your coming Reign and its righteousness as a standard. Help us to adjust our lives accordingly: that, our values realigned to your will, we may live lives that are holy in your sight and worthy of thanksgiving in ours. In the name of Jesus we pray. Amen

Prayer of Confession

God of bounty and blessing, it grieves us to confess that we have not always adopted your priority of things spiritual over things material, and that we have thus not treasured your greatest provisions to us, or given thanks for the most important of our blessings. Forgive us, we pray; help us to reorder our lives around the righteousness that you have given us by grace, and the Reign that you yet have in store; and convince us that everything else in our lives will then be properly arranged according to your will in Christ Jesus. In his name we pray. Amen

Scripture Index

Genesis
2:4b-9, 15-17, 25:—3:7	72
12:1-4a (4B-8)	75
12:1-9	138
22:1-18	141
25:19-34	144
28:10-17	147
32:22-32	150

Exodus
1:6-14, 22—2:10	153
2:11-22	156
3:1-12	159
3:13-20	162
12:1-14	102
12:1-14	165
14:19-31	168
16:2-15	171
17:1-7	174
17:3-7	78
19:1-9	177
19:16-24	180
20:1-20	183
24:12-18	66
32:1-14	186
33:12-23	189

Leviticus
19:1-2, 9-18	63

Numbers
6:22-27	33
27:12-23	192

Deuteronomy
4:32-40	135
30:15-20	57
34:1-12	195

Ruth
1:1-19a	198
2:1-13	201
4:7-17	204

1 Samuel
16:1-13	81

1 Kings
8:55-61	219

Isaiah
2:1-5	9
7:10-16	18
9:1-4	48
9:2-7	21
11:1-10	12
35:1-10	15
42:1-9	42, 93
44:1-8	132
49:1-7	45, 96
49:8-13	60
50:4-9a	87, 90, 99
52:7-10	27
52:13—53:12	105
58:3-9a	54
60:1-6	39
62:6-7, 10-12	24
63:7-9	30

Jeremiah
31:7-14	36

Ezekiel
34:11-16, 20-24	213
37:1-14	84

Joel
2:1-2, 12-17a	69

Amos
  5:18-24 — 207

Micah
  6:1-8 — 51

Zephaniah
  1:7, 12-18 — 210

Matthew
  1:18-25 — 20
  2:1-12 — 41
  2:13-15, 19-23 — 32
  3:1-12 — 14
  3:13-17 — 44
  4:1-11 — 74
  4:12-23 — 50
  5:1-12 — 53, 218
  5:13-16 — 56
  5:17-26 — 59
  5:27-37 — 62
  5:38-48 — 65
  6:1-6, 16-21 — 71
  6:25-33 — 221
  7:21-28 — 140
  9:9-13 — 143
  9:35—10:8 — 146
  10:24-33 — 149
  10:34-42 — 152
  11:2-11 — 17
  11:25-30 — 155
  13:1-9, 18-23 — 158
  13:24-30, 36-43 — 161
  13:44-52 — 164
  14:13-21 — 167
  14:22-33 — 170
  15:21-28 — 173
  16:13-20 — 176
  16:21-28 — 179
  17:1-9 — 68
  18:15-20 — 182
  18:21-35 — 185
  20:1-16 — 188
  21:1-11 — 92

Matthew *(continued)*
  21:28-32 — 191
  21:33-43 — 194
  22:1-14 — 197
  22:15-22 — 200
  23:1-12 — 206
  24:36-44 — 11
  24:22-46 — 203
  25:1-13 — 209
  25:14-30 — 212
  25:31-46 — 215
  26:14—27:66 — 89
  28:1-10 — 110
  28:16-20 — 137

Luke
  2:1-20 — 23
  2:8-20 — 26
  2:15-21 — 35
  24:13-35 — 116
  24:46-53 — 128

John
  1:1-14 — 29
  1:1-18 — 38
  1:29-34 — 47
  3:1-17 — 77
  4:5-26 — 80
  9:1-41 — 83
  10:1-10 — 119
  11:(1-16) 17-45 — 86
  12:1-11 — 95
  12:20-36 — 98
  13:1-15 — 104
  13:21-30 — 101
  14:1-14 — 122
  14:15-21 — 125
  17:1-11 — 131
  18:1—19:42 — 107
    (or 19:17-30)
  20:19-23 — 134
  20:19-31 — 113

Acts
1:1-11	126
1:6-14	129
2:1-21	133
2:14a, 22-32	111
2:14a, 36-41	114
2:42-47	117
7:55-60	120
10:34-43	43, 108
17:22-31	123

Romans
1:1-7	19
3:21-28	139
4:1-5 (6-12), 13-17	76
4:13-18	142
5:1-11	79
5:6-11	145
5:12-19	73, 148
6:3-11	151
7:14-25a	154
8:6-11	85
8:9-17	157
8:18-25	160
8:26-30	163
8:31-39	166
9:1-5	169
11:13-16, 29-32	172
11:33-36	175
12:1-13	178
13:1-10	181
13:11-14	10
14:5-12	184
15:4-13	13

1 Corinthians
1:1-9	46
1:3-9	220
1:10-17	49
1:18-31	52, 97
2:1-11	55
3:1-9	58
3:10-11, 16-23	61

1 Corinthians *(continued)*
4:1-5	64
11:23-26	103
15:20-28	214

2 Corinthians
5:20b—6:2 (3-10)	70

Ephesians
1:3-6, 15-18	37
1:15-23	127
3:1-12	40
5:8-14	82

Philippians
1:21-27	187
2:1-13	190
2:5-11	88, 91
2:9-13	34
3:12-21	193
4:1-9	196

Colossians
3:1-4	109

1 Thessalonians
1:1-10	199
2:1-8	202
2:9-13, 17-20	205
4:13-18	208
5:1-11	211

Titus
2:11-14	22
3:4-7	25

Hebrews
1:1-12	28
2:10-18	31
4:14-16, 5:7-9	106
9:11-15	94
12:1-3	100

James
5:7-10 — 16

1 Peter
1:3-9 — 112
1:17-23 — 115
2:2-10 — 121
2:19-25 — 118
3:13-22 — 124
4:12-14, 5:6-11 — 130

2 Peter
1:16-21 — 67

1 John
3:1-3 — 217

Revelation
7:9-17 — 216

About the Author

Dr. Paul A. Laughlin is a native of Covington, Kentucky (Greater Cincinnati) and a Phi Beta Kappa graduate of the University of Cincinnati. He obtained his Master of Divinity degree and his Ph.D. in Historical Theology from Emory University, Atlanta, Georgia, where he held the Dempster Fellowship. A United Methodist Minister, Dr. Laughlin has served as a pastor in Georgia and Kentucky, has taught at several colleges and seminaries, and is now Associate Professor of Religion and Philosophy at Otterbein College, Westerville, Ohio. He is also the founder and director of The Liturgical Jazz/Arts Ensemble, which since 1971 has led contemporary, multimedia worship services and workshops all over the South and Midwest. He and his wife Elizabeth have a five-year-old son, Drew.